T0316397

PRACTITIONERS' GUIDE TO MANAGERIAL ECONOMICS

2nd edition

Semoon Chang

UNIVERSITY
PRESS OF
AMERICA

Lanham • New York • London

Copyright © 1994 by
University Press of America,® Inc.
4720 Boston Way
Lanham, Maryland 20706

3 Henrietta Street
London WC2E 8LU England

Library of Congress Cataloging-in-Publication Data

Chang, Semoon.
Practitioners' guide to managerial economics /
Semoon Chang. — 2nd ed.
p.   cm.
Rev. ed. of: Principles of managerial economics /
J. Ronnie Davis, Semoon Chang. ©1986.
Includes bibliographical references and index.
1. Managerial economics.   I. Davis, J. Ronnie. Principles of
managerial economics.   II. Title.
HD30.22.C45   1994   338.5'024658—dc20   94–28353 CIP

ISBN 0–8191–9652–5 (pbk. : alk. paper)

 The paper used in this publication meets the minimum requirements of
American National Standard for Information Sciences—Permanence
of Paper for Printed Library Materials, ANSI Z39.48–1984.

Table of Contents

Part I Topics in Foundation

Table of Contents

List of Tables

List of Figures

Preface

Alimony is a payment made to a former spouse upon divorce, while palimony is a payment of support to a former cohabitant to whom one was not married. The legal recognition of palimony varies with individual states. In 1985, for instance, the Superior Court of New Jersey ruled that a woman could sue her deceased lover's estate for posthumous palimony based on her allegation that her lover promised to support her the rest of her life.

In 1984, the Mississippi Supreme Court declined to recognize palimony for Margie who had lived with Sam over 33 years and buried him on her mother's lot. The Mississippi Supreme Court offered the following seven reasons for the denial of the palimony: The parties could have drawn a will; cohabitation is looked upon with disfavor; cohabitation is against public policy; the acts performed by the person seeking the support payment were done gratuitously; to allow palimony would be to revive common law marriage in Mississippi; in effect, Margie was a mistress not a spouse; and the legislature, not the court, should decide the issue. This story is based on Ernest W. King, "Posthumous palimony: New Jersey takes the next step; Will Mississippi take the first step?" *Business Insights*, 6 (Fall 1986), 5-6.

It suffices here to point out that cohabitation without marriage or prenuptial agreements incurs an opportunity cost that can be measured by the amount that the surviving partner could have received if she or he were married to the deceased partner or made a prenuptial agreement with the deceased partner.

No less expensive than Margie's lost palimony is the price of a textbook. As discussed in Chapter 14 of this book, when payments are made by a third party (students), the demand for the product (textbooks) tends to be less elastic and publishers of the textbook increase the price for more profits for themselves as well as professors who write the textbook. This book is prepared to reverse the trend by keeping the cost of production low without sacrificing the quality. The quality, I believe, is higher because of my experience in having published similar textbooks in recent years. Fats are trimmed, but essential quantitative methods in differentiation and regression are preserved. Pages are reduced and hard-binding is avoided, but all important concepts and techniques are covered succinctly. Figures in this book are prepared by graduate assistant Say Hock Ng.

Semoon Chang
Mobile, Alabama

Chapter 1

Introduction

As best as it can be remembered, this is the story Earle Nightingale told his radio audience on May 11, 1988, through CBS radio affiliates: There was a flood in a small town. It was a bad flood, sweeping away practically everything in its path. One man was barely surviving on the roof of his home. When a boat came by whose operator asked the man to jump in, the man waved the boat off saying that he was a religious person and that God would save him. While he was praying, another boat came by and the man waved this boat off also, saying again that God would save him. Later, a helicopter hovered above him and was dropping a rope for him to climb up. The man waved the helicopter off, however, telling the crew not to worry since God would save him. He drowned. Later he was standing at the gate of Heaven, and he asked the gatekeeper why God did not save him. The gatekeeper responded, "Didn't you have two boats and a helicopter trying to save you?"

In a sense, studying economics is like the man in the story searching for two boats and a helicopter sent by God. There must be more knowledge that can help us improve the way we manage the economy, and private businesses as well. It is highly possible that the knowledge is already here but we simply do not recognize it. In economics, we continue to pursue the knowledge through scientific thinking so that we can avoid the danger of being drowned.

Formally stated, **economics** is a science used to study aspects of human behavior that deal with the relationship between given wants and scarce resources that have alternative uses. The key word in the definition of economics is the **scarcity** or shortage of resources that can be used for production of alternative products. Whenever there is a shortage of resources that requires their allocation among alternative uses, there is an economic problem. One assumption that underlies all business decision-making is that there is a shortage of resources, forcing managers to economize on use of resources. Making business decisions is an economic problem.

The Process of Optimization

The root of all economic problems is the scarcity of resources that makes rationing of resources unavoidable. The process of rationing scarce resources among alternative uses in order to attain some well-defined objective is referred to as **optimization**. Optimization underlies most, if not all, economic problems. In production, managers of plants optimize the use of resources by trying to produce a maximum quantity of output with given resources or produce a given quantity of output with minimum resources. In distribution, managers of firms optimize the use of transportation resources by trying to select a combination of different modes of transportation so that the total delivery cost can be minimized. In consumption, consumers optimize the use of their budget by trying to purchase and consume a combination of goods and services that will give them the most satisfaction with a given budget.

Hypothesis, Assumption, and Theory

To understand what the scientific method is all about, several terms need to be clarified. These terms include assumption, hypothesis, model, and theory.

A **hypothesis** is a proposition tentatively assumed in order to test its truthfulness against facts that are known or may be determined. In case of hypotheses that explore historical data, it is possible to find facts that predictions indicated by the hypothesis retroactively confirm. In the June 1, 1987 issue of Newsweek (p. 8), Fred Brock suggested that "the level of enrollment in a course correlates in inverse proportion to the level of intellectual energy required to pass it." This quotation is an example of a hypothesis, assuming that it is not yet proven to be true.

Stating assumptions is important in developing hypotheses. An **assumption** is the act of taking for granted or supposing that a thing is true. An assumption is also something that is taken for granted. Some assumptions are so obvious that they are, for all practical purposes, tautologies, or needless repetitions.

The number of both obvious and less obvious assumptions that can be stated for a given hypothesis is virtually endless. We in economics, therefore, use an expression, *ceteris paribus*, in order to hold constant all factors that may affect the test of a hypothesis but are not stated explicitly. **Ceteris paribus** means "all other things being equal."

What is a theory? A **theory** may be defined as a hypothesis whose truthfulness has already been proven empirically. Theory, thus defined, requires observation of facts to support the claim made by the theory. Sometimes, theory and hypothesis are used interchangeably. A theory may be expressed in a model. A **model** is usually a system of equations that represent a theory. The terms, model and theory, are also used interchangeably.

An Illustration

Professor David Phillips wanted to test a hypothesis that a person's death month is related to the birth month in that some people postpone death in order to witness their birthdays. To test the hypothesis, the birth and death dates of more than 1,200 famous people were examined. The study found a decrease in the number of deaths before the birth month and an increase in the number of deaths after the birth month. The dips and the rises in the number of deaths were much more than what might reasonably be explained by chance. The study also found that the more famous a group of individuals under investigation was, the larger were the death dips of its members before birthdays and their death rises after birthdays.

According to Phillips, some people postpone their death in order to witness events other than their birthdays.[1] There are fewer deaths than expected before the Jewish Day of Atonement in New York, where a large Jewish population resides. There is a dip in U.S. deaths before U.S. presidential elections. Both Jefferson and Adams died on July 4, 1825, fifty years after the Declaration of Independence was signed. Jefferson's last words as quoted by his physician were "Is it the Fourth?"

Following Chapters

This book is divided into four parts. Part I presents the supply and demand model, and the coverage of quantitative methods. Following Chapter 2 on supply and demand, Chapter 3 summarizes rules of differentiation and optimization, while Chapters 4 and 5 present the principles of applied regression analysis.

Generic managerial economic topics are presented in Parts II and III. Three chapters in Part II explain basic microeconomic concepts such as elasticities, production, and costs of production. Presented in the four chapters of Part III are topics on market structure and price and output decisions of firms under perfection competition (Chapter 9), monopoly (Chapter 10), monopolistic competition and oligopoly (Chapter 11), and market failures and antitrust laws (Chapter 12).

Selected topics of interest to business managers and economists are discussed in Part IV. Forecasting is presented in Chapter 13; pricing and profit analysis in Chapter 14; and capital budgeting as well as consultants' favorite topic feasibility studies are presented in Chapter 15.

End Notes

1.   David P. Phillips, Deathday and birthday: "An unexpected connection," in Judith M. Tanur (ed.), *Statistics: A guide to the unknown*, (San Francisco: Holden-Day, 1972), pp. 52-65.

Chapter 2

Demand, Supply, and Market Equilibrium

In a market economy, competition works through the interaction of supply and demand. Individual sellers pursue private interests by selling the quantity and charging the price that will maximize their profits. Individual buyers, on the other hand, pursue private interests by selecting the bundle of goods and services that will maximize their satisfaction. There is no order imposed from above, but there is a sense of orderliness in the market. A **market** is an arrangement in which sellers of a good or service interact with buyers of the good or service.

What Is Demand?

Demand is said to exist when consumers capable of paying for a good or service are willing to buy the good or service in order to satisfy their wants. **Market demand** refers to the quantities of a good or service that are demanded by all buyers in any given market at various prices. A schedule that shows the relation between different prices and the quantities demanded at these prices in a market is called a market demand schedule.

Law of Demand

At any given time, there is a definite relation between the price of a good or service and its quantity demanded. The relation is inverse, which means that as the price of a good or service increases, the quantity of the good or service demanded is expected to decrease. Also, as the price of a good or service decreases, the quantity of the good or service demanded is expected to increase. This inverse relation between the price of a product and the quantity of the product demanded is observed with such regularity that it is called the **law of demand.**

Demand Function

   A function is a relation between the dependent variable and one or more independent variables. For instance, if

$$y = f(x) \qquad\qquad (2\text{-}1)$$

y is the dependent variable and x is the independent variable. Equation (2-1) means that the value of y depends on the value of x. Equation (2-1) is a general expression that y depends on x. It does not tell us how x and y are related. A simple, but a clearer, relation between x and y is a linear function:

$$y = a + bx \qquad\qquad (2\text{-}2)$$

In equation (2-2), the value of y is "a" when the value of x is zero, and the value of y increases by "b" as the value of x increases by 1. The "+" sign in front of "b" means that as the value of x increases, the value of y also increases. The variables x and y are directly or positively related.
   By replacing "y" by P and "x" by Q_D, equation (2-2) is transformed to a demand function in which P is the price of the product and Q_D is the quantity of the product demanded. Due to the law of demand, however, we need to change the "+" sign into a "-" sign:

$$P = a - bQ_D \qquad\qquad (2\text{-}3)$$

Some economists prefer to call (2-3) an equation for a demand curve or simply a demand curve in order to differentiate (2-3) from a demand function that contains Q_D as the dependent variable.

Suppose that

$$P = 110 - 2Q_D \qquad (2\text{-}4)$$

In (2-4), consumers buy nothing ($Q_D = 0$) when price is 110, while consumers take 55 units if the product is given away free;

$$\text{At } Q_D = 0, P = 110 - 2(0) = 110$$
$$\text{At } P = 0, 0 = 110 - 2Qd$$
$$Q_D = 55$$

What Is Supply?

Supply refers to the quantities of a good or service that a seller is willing and able to make available for sale in the market at various prices. **Market supply** is a summation of all supply schedules of individual firms in any given market.

Law of Supply

At any given time, there is a definite relation between the price of a good or service and its quantity supplied. The relation is direct. This direct relation between the price of a product and the quantity of the product supplied, although observed with less regularity than the law of demand, is called the **law of supply**.

Supply Function

A supply function is an algebraic expression of the law of supply. By replacing "y" by P and "x" by Q_S in equation (2-2), the equation is transformed to a supply function. Q_S is the quantity of the product supplied and P is the price of the product. Since the price and the quantity supplied are positive related, we do not have to change the " + " sign:

$$P = a + bQ_s \qquad (2\text{-}5)$$

Again, some economists prefer to call (2-5) an equation for a supply curve or simply a supply curve in order to differentiate (2-5) from a supply function that contains Q_s as the dependent variable.

Suppose that

$$P = 10 + 3Q_s \qquad (2\text{-}6)$$

In (2-6), businesses no longer want to sell any when price is 10, while businesses want to sell 30 units when price is \$100;

$$\text{At } P = 10, \quad 10 = 10 + 3Q_s$$
$$Q_s = 0$$
$$\text{At } P = 100, \quad 100 = 10 + 3Q_s$$
$$90 = 3Q_s$$
$$Q_s = 30$$

Market Equilibrium

If demand is one blade of the scissors that is the market, market supply is the other. Just as the two blades of a scissors must work together to cut paper, so are the price of a product and the quantity of the product traded in the market determined only if information is available on both market demand and market supply.

Equilibrium in Graph

In any given market, demand for a good or service interacts with supply of the good or service, resulting in a price that clears the market. **Clearing the market** means that the price equates the quantity demanded and the quantity supplied for a given good or service. The price that equates the quantity of a product demanded and the quantity of the product supplied is called the **equilibrium price**. The quantity exchanged at the equilibrium price is called the **equilibrium quantity**.

Equilibrium means an equality between opposing forces. In a market equilibrium, the opposing forces acting on price are balanced, so that there is no tendency for the price to move up or down. The market equilibrium is achieved through a balancing act between too much demand, which tends to raise price, and too much supply, which tends to lower price.

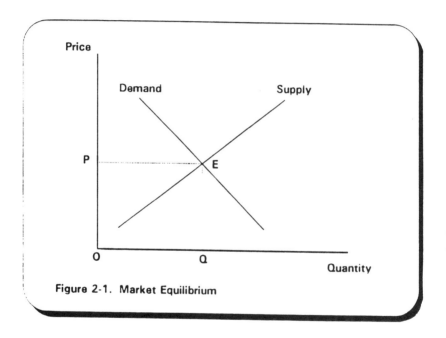

Figure 2-1. Market Equilibrium

The balancing act between demand function (2-4) and supply function (2-6) is graphically generalized in Figure (2-1). The crossing point E between demand and supply schedules is the point of equilibrium. The equilibrium price (P) and the equilibrium quantity traded (Q) are found by extending a line from point E to the vertical price line and the horizontal quantity line.

Equilibrium in Algebra

   The exact equilibrium price and quantity may be obtained algebraical-
ly. Given,

$$P = 110 - 2Q_D \qquad\qquad (2\text{-}4)$$
$$P = 10 + 3Q_s \qquad\qquad (2\text{-}6)$$

there are only one price and one quantity at the equilibrium point. We,
therefore, replace Q_D in equation (2-4) and Q_s in equation (2-6) by Q,
and solve the two equations simultaneously:

$$P = 110 - 2Q \qquad\qquad (2\text{-}4')$$
$$P = 10 + 3Q \qquad\qquad (2\text{-}6')$$

Since P = P,

$$110 - 2Q = 10 + 3Q$$
$$100 = 5Q$$
$$Q = 20$$

Plugging Q = 20 into equation (2-4') or (2-6'),

$$P = 110 - 2(20)$$
$$P = 70$$

Shifts in Demand and Supply Curves

   In presenting a simple demand and supply model, it was assumed that
the quantity (Q) of a product demanded or supplied depended on the
price (P) of the product alone. We thus treated Q as the dependent
variable and P as an independent variable. In graphs, the dependent
variable is shown on the vertical line and the independent variable is
shown on the horizontal line. In demand and supply model, however, we
show price on the vertical line and quantity on the horizontal line. To

draw demand and supply curves, we used P as the dependent variable and Q as an independent variable in equations (2-3) and (2-5). In this section, we return to the original demand and supply functions in which Q_D or Q_S is the dependent variable in order to generalize these functions.

Demand Function Revisited

In reality, the quantity of a good or service demanded depends on many factors in addition to the price of the good or service. These factors include money income of consumers (Y), taste or preference of consumers regarding the good or service (T), number of consumers in a given market (N), prices of goods and services that are related to the good or service under consideration (P_R) and other determinants like the education level of consumers, age, types of neighbors, and more. Stated in algebraic form, the relation between the quantity of a good or service, called X, demanded and its determinants is expressed as

$$Q_X = f(P_X; Y, T, N, P_R). \qquad (2-7)$$

Let us find out the exact relations between the quantity of product X demanded and the factors that influence the quantity.

The relation between the price of product X and the quantity of product X demanded is inverse. This relation was explained as the law of demand.

The relation between demand for product X and consumers' income is direct. When demand for a good or service increases as income rises, the good or service is called a **normal or superior good**. Demand for certain goods or services decreases as income rises. These goods or services are called **inferior goods**. Inferior goods have preferred substitutes that are more expensive. A good may be an inferior good to one person, but a normal good to another person.

Demand for product X will increase as more consumers come to like the product. The relation between demand for product X and its taste or preference (T) is expected to be direct. Also, as the number of consumers of product X increases in a given market, demand for the product is expected to increase. The relation between demand for product X and the number of consumers is expected to be direct.

There are two types of goods or services that are related to product X: substitutes and complements. **Substitutes** are products other than product X that can satisfy human wants almost as well as product X does. As the price of a substitute for product X decreases, the demand for product X is expected to decrease as well, since more consumers will buy the substitute, which is now cheaper. **Complements** are goods or services that are used together. Unlike substitutes, the relation between the price of a complement to product X and the demand for product X itself is expected to be inverse. As the price of a complement decreases, the demand for product X is expected to increase, since the lower price of a complement means a lower total cost of consuming product X and its complement.

Substitution Effect and Income Effect

When the price of product X falls and prices of other products are unchanged, consumers of the product X respond to this change in two ways. First, consumers may substitute some quantity of the relatively cheaper product for other relatively more expensive products. This is known as the **substitution effect**. Second, consumers are able to buy greater quantities of the relatively cheaper product as well as greater quantities of other relatively more expensive products with the same income, since the same income can now buy more with the fall in the price of product X. This second effect is known as the **income effect**.

When the price of a normal good falls, both substitution and income effects lead consumers to buy a greater quantity of the good. When the price of an inferior good falls, substitution effect leads consumers to buy a greater quantity, but income effect leads consumers to buy a smaller quantity of the good. The net effect is still likely an increased quantity of the good demanded. If, however, the income effect that works against buying a greater quantity of an inferior good outweighs the substitution effect, a falling price may actually lead to a decreased quantity of the good demanded. If this happens, the product is called the **Giffen good**, named after a 19th century British civil servant.

The **Giffen's paradox** represents an exception to the law of demand and occurs only if the inverse income effect of an inferior good is stronger than the substitution effect.

Shifts in Demand Curve

Rewriting demand function (2-7) according to the relations between the quantity of X demanded and its determinants:

$$Q_X = a - bP_X + cY + dT + eN \pm P_R \qquad (2\text{-}8)$$

The sign for P_R can be "+" for substitutes or "-" for complements.

In graphing a demand curve, only price (P) and quantity (Q) are shown. All other variables in (2-8) are assumed to remain unchanged. These other variables become part of the constant as indicated in (2-9):

$$Q_X = A - bP_X \qquad (2\text{-}9)$$

where $A = a + cY + dT + eN \pm P_R$

To draw a demand curve, equation (2-9) is solved for P_X as the dependent variable:

$$P_X = (A/b) - (1/b)Q_X \qquad (2\text{-}10)$$

Equation (2-10) indicates that changes in Y, T, N, and P_R affect the value of the constant term A while leaving the slope of the demand curve (-1/b) unchanged. Put differently, changes in, or any combinations of, Y, T, N, and P_R will shift the demand curve. The demand curve shifts to the right, if consumers' income increases, more consumers like the product, more consumers move into the market, prices of substitutes rise, or if prices of complements fall. The demand curve shifts to the left, if consumers' income decreases, less consumers like the product, more consumers leave the market, prices of substitutes fall, or if prices of complements rise.

When the demand curve shifts, there is a *change in demand*. The change can be an increase in which the demand curve shifts to the right, or a decrease in which the demand curve shifts to the left. If there is a change in the price of the product itself, the demand curve remains the same. In this case, there is a *change in quantity demanded*.

Supply Function Revisited

In drawing a supply curve, it was assumed that the quantity of a good or service supplied depended on the price of the good or service alone. In reality, the quantity of a product supplied depends on many factors in addition to the price of the product. These determinants include resource prices (R), production technology (H), and other such determinants as taxes and subsidies and the number of sellers (O) in a given market. Stated in algebraic form, the relation between the quantity of a good or service supplied and its determinants may be expressed as

$$Q_X = f(P_X; R, H, O). \qquad (2\text{-}11)$$

Let us determine the exact relations between the quantity of product X supplied and the factors that influence the quantity of product X supplied. The relation between the price of product X and the quantity of product X supplied is direct. This relation was explained as the law of supply.

Supply of a product presupposes its production. The production of a product typically requires the use of several resources. These resources are called input factors, or simply inputs. If prices of resources decrease while the price of the product remains unchanged, the profit of the producer increases, motivating the producer to increase the supply of the product. The relation between the supply of a product and resource prices is inverse.

An improvement in production technology has the same effect as a decrease in resource prices. Assuming that the product price remains unchanged, an improvement in production technology increases the profit of the producer, motivating the producer to increase the supply of the product. The relation between the supply of a product and production technology is also is direct.

Shifts in Supply Curve

Rewriting supply function (2-11) according to the relations between the quantity of X supplied and its determinants:

$$Q_X = a + bP_X - cR + dH \quad (2\text{-}12)$$

In graphing a supply curve, only price (P) and quantity (Q) are shown. All other variables in (2-12) are assumed to remain unchanged. These other variables become part of the constant as indicated in (2-13):

$$Q_X = A + bP_X \quad (2\text{-}13)$$

where $A = a - cR + dH$

To draw a supply curve, equation (2-13) is solved for P_X as the dependent variable:

$$P_X = -(A/b) + (1/b)Q_X \quad (2\text{-}14)$$

Equation (2-14) indicates that changes in R and H affect the value of the constant term A while leaving the slope of the supply curve $(+1/b)$ unchanged. Put differently, changes in, or any combinations of, R and H will shift the supply curve. The supply curve shifts to the right if input prices fall or production technology improves, and *vice versa*.

When the supply curve shifts, there is a *change in supply*. The change can be an increase in which the supply curve shifts to the right, or a decrease in which the supply curve shifts to the left. If there is a change in the price of the product itself, the supply curve remains the same. In this case, there is a *change in quantity supplied*.

An Illustration

A *linear* estimation of demand function is rare but exists.[1] The demand function for national brand frozen concentrated orange juice (FCOJ), estimated by Lee, Brown, and Schwartz, is simplified below with price as the only independent variable:

$$Q_D = 11.5 - 0.3301P \qquad (2\text{-}15)$$

where Q_D is the quantity of FCOJ in ounces purchased per person during the person's weekly shopping trip and P is the price per ounce of FCOJ.

The law of supply does not work as well as the law of demand, explaining in part why there is such a paucity of estimated supply functions. The supply function in (2-16) is a hypothetical supply function derived in such a way as to generate the price and the quantity of FCOJ exchanged as indicated in the study by Lee, Brown, and Schwartz. The hypothetical supply function is

$$Q_S = -4.6 + 1.5P \qquad (2\text{-}16)$$

Solving for the equilibrium price and quantity,

$$
\begin{aligned}
Q_D &= Q_S \\
11.5 - 0.3301P &= -4.6 + 1.5P \\
1.8301P &= 16.1 \\
P &= \$8.88 \\
Q &= 11.5 - 0.3301(8.88) \text{ or} \\
&= -4.6 + 1.5(8.88) \\
&= 8.72 \text{ oz.}
\end{aligned}
$$

Summary

Market demand refers to the quantities of a product that are demanded by all buyers in any given market at various prices. There is an inverse relation between the price of a product and the quantity of the product demanded. The inverse relation is called the law of demand. Market supply is a summation of all supply schedules of individual firms in any given market. The direct relation between the price of a product and the quantity of the product supplied is called the law of supply. At equilibrium price, the quantity of a product demanded is equal to the quantity of the product supplied.

The quantity of a product demanded depends on many factors including the price of the product, money income of consumers, taste or preference of consumers, number of consumers in a given market, prices of goods and services that are related to the good or service under consideration, and more. When demand for a product increases as income rises, the product is called a normal or superior good, while products that decrease as income rises are called inferior goods. Inferior goods have preferred substitutes that are more expensive. Substitutes are products that can satisfy human wants almost equally, while complements are goods or services that are used together. If there is a change in the price of a given product, there is a change in quantity of the product demanded and the demand curve remains the same. If there is a change in any determinant other than the price of the product, there is a change in demand and the demand curve shifts.

When the price of a product falls and prices of other products are unchanged, consumers of the product may substitute some quantity of the relatively cheaper product for other relatively more expensive products. This is the substitution effect. When the price of a product falls, consumers are able to buy greater quantities of the relatively cheaper product as well as greater quantities of other relatively more expensive products with the same income. This is the income effect. If the income effect of an inferior good outweighs the substitution effect, a falling price may actually lead to a decreased quantity of the good demanded. If this happens, the product is called the Giffen good.

End Notes

1.   Jong-Ying Lee, Mark G. Brown, and Brooke Schwartz (1986), "The demand for national brand and private label frozen concen-

trated orange juice: A switching regression analysis," a working paper by the Florida Agricultural Experiment Station, 1986, published later in Western Journal of Agricultural Economics, 11 (July 1986), 1-7.

Chapter 3

Optimization Concepts and Techniques

A business decision frequently involves considering a large number of options and then choosing the best alternative. A manager may consider production at different levels of output and then choose the level at which a largest amount of profit is expected from sales. This is a maximization problem. A manager may also consider different combinations of inputs that can produce a given level of output and then choose the combination that is expected to be least costly. This is a minimization problem. Decision making that involves solutions of maximization and minimization problems is called **optimization**. In a sense, the entire decision making process in business world is the optimization process.

The study of optimization can be made easier if we use simple rules of differentiation.

From First Derivative to Marginal

Consider Figure (3-1) in which total cost (TC) is shown to depend on the quantity of output (Q). The total cost is intentionally drawn as a rapidly rising curve to the right in order to demonstrate the concept of a derivative.

In Figure 3-1, the total cost of producing the quantity of output OQ_1 is EQ_1, while the total cost of producing OQ_2 is AQ_2. As the quantity of output increases from OQ_1 to OQ_2, total cost increases from DQ_2 (which is equal to EQ_1) to AQ_2. Since total cost is increased by AD (which is the difference between AQ_2 and DQ_2) as the quantity of output increases by ED (which is equal to Q_1Q_2), we can obtain marginal cost (MC) by dividing increases in total cost AD by increases in the quantity of output ED:

$$MC = AD/ED \qquad\qquad (3\text{-}1)$$

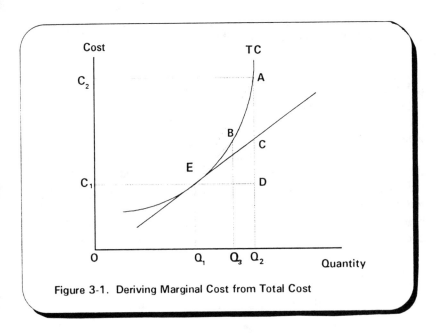

Figure 3-1. Deriving Marginal Cost from Total Cost

When a vertical distance AD is divided by a horizontal distance ED in (3-1), a slope is obtained. Expression (3-1), therefore, can be restated as

$$MC = \angle AED \qquad\qquad (3\text{-}2)$$

The marginal cost of increasing the quantity of output by ED is slope

AED.

We now ask ourselves an interesting question: What happens if we measure the marginal cost by slope CED in which line CE is tangent to the total cost curve at point E? Perhaps, a better question is: Why do we want to do that? So long as we start from point E for quantity OQ_1, there is only one line that is tangent to total cost curve at point E and thus slope CED is stable. In comparison, slope AED changes as the quantity of output changes. If this answer is not convincing, let us move on.

If we do measure marginal cost by slope CED rather than the actual slope AED, there is an error measured by the difference between the two slopes, which is slope AEC. If we somehow reduce the slope AEC, then the error is also reduced. We can reduce the slope AEC by making the increase in the quantity of output smaller, say, from OQ_2 to OQ_3. At OQ_3, the marginal cost is measured by slope BED and the difference between the actual marginal cost and the slope CED that we want to use to measure the marginal cost is reduced from $\angle$ AEC to $\angle$ BEC. To generalize, the smaller the incremental quantity of output is, the more accurate the slope CED is in measuring the marginal cost at OQ_1 level of output.

We may formalize this general statement by using algebraic symbols:

$$\lim_{\Delta Q=0} \frac{\Delta TR}{\Delta Q} = \frac{dTC}{dQ} \qquad (3\text{-}3)$$

In (3-3), "lim" stands for limit, indicating that Q changes but only by an infinitesimally small amount. Then, $\Delta TC/\Delta Q$ becomes dTC/dQ, which is read as the first derivative of TC with respect to Q. Q has to change even by an infinitesimally small amount in order to have a marginal cost, since marginal cost by definition is a change in total cost divided by a change in the quantity of output.

To summarize, the first derivative of total cost function measures marginal cost as indicated in (3-3); measures the slope of the total cost function as defined in (3-2); and measures the rate of change in total cost as the quantity of output changes by one unit as shown in (3-1). The first derivative always measures the rate of change, the slope, or the marginal value of a total function, regardless of whether the total function is total cost, total revenue, total profit, or any other total function. Any time derivatives dTC/dQ appear imposing, convert the expression to $\Delta TC/\Delta Q$, which makes it less imposing to interpret the derivatives. Keeping these interpretations in mind, we introduce rules of differentiation.

Rules of Differentiation

There area only a small number of rules of differentiation, introduced below, that are extensively used in business and economic analysis.[1]

Derivative of a Constant

The (first) derivative of a constant is zero, since a constant is graphed as a horizontal line that has zero slope. In algebraic terms, consider "y" as the dependent variable and "x" as an independent variable, $y = f(x)$. by taking the derivative, we are evaluating the impact of a change in "x" on the value of "y". If the independent variable is a constant "k" so that

$$y = k, \qquad\qquad (3\text{-}4)$$

changes in "x" will have no impact on "k" since "k" is a constant:

$$dy/dx = 0 \qquad\qquad (3\text{-}5)$$

or

$$y' = 0. \qquad\qquad (3\text{-}6)$$

Examples of a constant function are the monthly fee for a cable TV that is unaffected by changes in viewing time, and a monthly apartment rent that includes an unlimited use of water. Changes in the amount of water that tenants use have no effect on the monthly rent.

Derivative of a Power Function

A power function is defined as

$$y = ax^b \qquad (3\text{-}7)$$

where "b" can be any number, "a" is the coefficient of the "x" term and the variable "x" is raised to the power "b". We take the derivative of a power function by moving the power "b" to the front and subtracting 1 from the power:

$$dy/dx = bax^{(b-1)} \qquad (3\text{-}8)$$

For example, if

$$y = 3x^2, \qquad (3\text{-}9)$$

then

$$dy/dx = (2)3x^{(2-1)} = 6x^1 = 6x. \qquad (3\text{-}10)$$

Also, if

$$y = 5x, \qquad (3\text{-}11)$$

which is the same as

$$y = 5x^1, \qquad (3\text{-}12)$$

then

$$dy/dx = (1)5x^{(1-1)} = 5x^0 = 5 \qquad (3\text{-}13)$$

since anything to the zero power is one.

Derivative of a Sum or a Difference

The derivative of a sum (or a difference) of two or more functions is the sum (or difference) of their separate derivatives. If

$$y = f(x) + g(x) \qquad (3\text{-}14)$$

then

$$dy/dx = df(x)/dx + dg(x)/dx \qquad (3\text{-}15)$$

which may also be expressed as

$$dy/dx = f'(x) + g'(x). \qquad (3\text{-}16)$$

Similarly, if

$$y = f(x) - g(x), \qquad (3\text{-}17)$$

then

$$y' = f'(x) - g'(x). \qquad (3\text{-}18)$$

For example, if we combine (3-4) and (3-9) so that

$$y = 10 + 3x^2, \qquad (3\text{-}19)$$

then the derivative of (3-19)

$$dy/dx = 0 + 6x. \qquad (3\text{-}20)$$

For another example, consider the profit function in which profit π is defined as total revenue minus total cost. Remember that both total revenue and total cost depend on the quantity of output. The profit function is stated as

$$\pi = TR(Q) - TC(Q) \qquad (3\text{-}21)$$

The derivative of the profit function with respect to changes in the quantity of output is

$$d\pi/dQ = TR'(Q) - TC'(Q) \qquad (3\text{-}22)$$

Since the first derivative of total revenue function is marginal revenue function and the first derivative of total cost function is marginal cost function, equation (3-22) is restated as

$$d\pi/dQ = MR(Q) - MC(Q) \qquad (3\text{-}23)$$

or

$$d\pi/dQ = MR - MC. \qquad (3\text{-}24)$$

Derivative of a Product

The derivative of the product of two functions is equal to the first function times the derivative of the second function, plus the second function times the derivative of the first function. That is, if

$$y = f(x)g(x) \qquad (3\text{-}25)$$

then

$$dy/dx = f(x)[dg(x)/dx] + g(x)[df(x)/dx] \qquad (3\text{-}26)$$

For example, consider

$$y = 3x^2(2x + 1) \qquad (3\text{-}27)$$

The derivative of (3-27) is

$$\begin{aligned} dy/dx &= 3x^2(2) + (6x)(2x + 1) \\ &= 18x^2 + 6x \end{aligned} \qquad (3\text{-}28)$$

Derivative of a Quotient

The derivative of the quotient of two functions is equal to the denominator times the derivative of the numerator, minus the numerator times the derivative of the denominator, all divided by the denominator squared. That is, if

$$y = \frac{f(x)}{g(x)} \qquad (3\text{-}29)$$

then, the derivative is

$$dy/dx = \frac{g(x)[df(x)/dx] - f(x)[dg(x)/dx]}{[g(x)]^2} \qquad (3\text{-}30)$$

For example, consider

$$y = \frac{2x + 1}{3x + 2} \qquad (3\text{-}31)$$

The derivative of (3-31) is

$$dy/dx = \frac{(3x + 2)2 - (2x + 1)3}{(3x + 2)^2}$$

$$= 1/(3x + 2)^2 \qquad (3\text{-}32)$$

Derivatives of Higher Order

The derivative of a derivative is called the second derivative of a function. Reconsider the power function (3-7)

$$y = ax^b \qquad (3\text{-}7)$$

The first derivative of (3-7) was

$$dy/dx = bax^{(b-1)} \qquad (3\text{-}8)$$

The second derivative of (3-7) is the first derivative of (3-8), which is

$$d^2y/dx^2 = (b-1)bax^{(b-2)} \qquad (3\text{-}33)$$

or

$$y'' = (b-1)bax^{(b-2)} \qquad (3-34)$$

The second derivative measures the slope, or the rate of change of the first derivative. Derivatives of a higher order have few applications in managerial economics and thus are not presented.

As an example of taking the second derivative, reconsider equation (3-19)

$$y = 10 + 3x^2, \qquad (3-19)$$

The first and second derivatives are

$$y' = 6x, \qquad (3-20)$$
$$y'' = 6. \qquad (3-35)$$

For another example, consider a quadratic equation

$$y = ax^2 + bx + c \qquad (3-36)$$

The first and second derivatives are

$$y' = 2ax + b \qquad (3-37)$$
$$y'' = 2a. \qquad (3-38)$$

For another example of the second derivative, consider profit function (3-21)

$$\pi = TR(Q) - TC(Q) \qquad (3-21)$$

The first derivative of the profit function is

$$d\pi/dQ = TR'(Q) - TC'(Q) \qquad (3-22)$$

or

$$d\pi/dQ = MR(Q) - MC(Q) \qquad (3-23)$$

The second derivative is

$$d^2\pi/dQ^2 = TR''(Q) - TC''(Q) \qquad (3-39)$$

or

$$d^2\pi/dQ^2 = MR'(Q) - MC'(Q) \qquad (3-40)$$

The first derivative of total revenue function was marginal revenue function. The second derivative of total revenue function measures the rate of change or the slope of the marginal revenue function. Likewise, the second derivative of the total cost function measures the rate of change or the slope of the marginal cost function.

Partial Derivatives

   The discussion of derivatives has been limited so far to functions of only one independent variable. In business and economics, however, the dependent variable such as the quantity of output may depend on the values of several variables such as labor and capital. Partial derivatives deal with functions of the general form that have more than one independent variable:

$$y = f(x_1, x_{2, ..,} x_n) \qquad (3-41)$$

In (3-41), the "x" variables are independent of one another. A change in one independent variable does not cause a change in any of the other independent variables.
   Through partial derivatives we measure the change in the dependent variable "y" in response to changes in one of the independent variables with all other independent variables remaining constant at fixed values. The symbol used to represent a partial derivative is

$$\partial y/\partial x_i \qquad (3-42)$$

which is read as the partial derivative of "y" with respect to x_i.
   For example, consider a two-independent variable function

$$y = 10 + 2x_1 + 3x_2 \qquad (3\text{-}43)$$

Since there are two independent variables, there can be two partial derivatives:

$$\partial y/\partial x_1 = 2 \qquad (3\text{-}44)$$
$$\partial y/\partial x_2 = 3 \qquad (3\text{-}45)$$

In (3-44), we take a partial derivative of "y" with respect to x_1 while keeping x_2 constant. The term $3x_2$, therefore, is treated as a constant just like the first term 10, and drops out. In (3-45), we take a partial derivative of "y" with respect to x_2 while keeping x_1 constant. The term $2x_1$ is treated as a constant just like the first term 10, and drops out.

For another example, consider a production function of the form

$$Q = AL^{\alpha}K^{\beta} \qquad (3\text{-}46)$$

in which Q is the quantity of output, while L and K represent units of labor and capital inputs respectively. The exponents, α and β, are the labor and capital coefficients. Since there are two independent variables L and K, there are two partial derivatives.

$$\partial Q/\partial L = \alpha AL^{(\alpha-1)}K^{\beta} \qquad (3\text{-}47)$$

$$\partial Q/\partial K = \beta AL^{\alpha}K^{(\beta-1)} \qquad (3\text{-}48)$$

In (3-47), we treat the capital input K constant but the expression K^{β} is not dropping out because it is an integral part of the entire right-side term $L^{\alpha}K^{\beta}$; it is not connected to L through a plus or minus sign. The partial derivative $\partial Q/\partial L$ in (3-47) measures a change in the quantity of output in response to changes in the labor input, and is called the marginal product of labor. The partial derivative $\partial Q/\partial K$ in (3-48) measures a change in the quantity of output in response to changes in the capital input, and is called the marginal product of capital.

Rules of Optimization

Optimization problems are concerned with variables under the control of business managers that maximize or minimize certain objective functions.

First and Second Derivatives Revisited

To understand the rules of optimization, we need to have a firm grasp of the difference between first derivatives and second derivatives in graphs. In Figure 3-2, "y" increases as "x" increases, indicating that the first derivative of "y" is positive. The rate of increase in "y", however, is indicated by the second derivative. If the second derivative is zero, "y" is graphed as a straight line in (b). The rate of change is constant in a straight line. If the second derivative is positive, "y" is increasing and

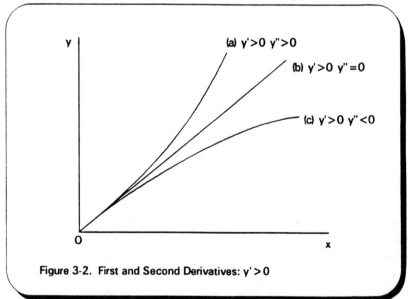

Figure 3-2. First and Second Derivatives: y' > 0

curved upward in (a), meaning that "y" increases at an increasing rate as "x" increases. If the second derivative is negative, "y" is still increasing but curved downward in (c), meaning that "y" increases at a decreasing rate.

In Figure 3-3, "y" decreases as "x" increases, indicating that the first derivative of "y" is negative. The rate of decrease in "y", however, is indicated by the second derivative. If the second derivative is zero, "y" is graphed as a straight line in (b). The rate of change is constant in a straight line. If the second derivative is positive, "y" is still decreasing but curved upward in (a), meaning that "y" decreases at an increasing rate as "x" increases. If the second derivative is negative, "y" is decreasing and curved downward in (c), meaning that "y" decreases at a decreasing rate.

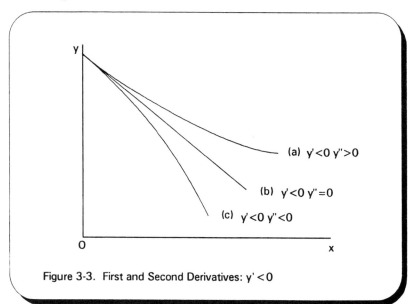

Figure 3-3. First and Second Derivatives: y' < 0

Optimization in Graph

In graphs, the optimization rules are easy to understand. In Figure 3-4, there are two curves; one dome-shaped and the other bowl-shaped. The highest point H in the dome has a zero slope, and thus $y' = 0$ at point H. The lowest point L in the bowl also has a zero slope, and thus $y' = 0$ at point L. The first derivative tells us that the optimal point can be either a maximum or a minimum, but does not tell us which one. To determine whether the optimal point is a maximum or a minimum, we need to look at the shape of the curve at points H and L. The shape of the curve is indicated by the second derivative.

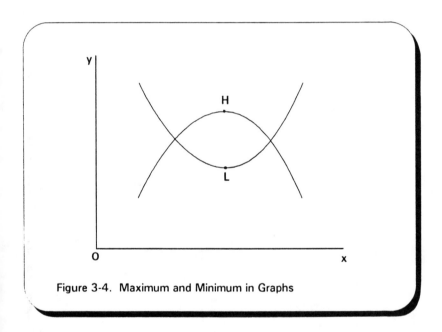

Figure 3-4. Maximum and Minimum in Graphs

Consider point H. The shape of the dome prior to point H is described by curve (c) in Figure 3-2, while the shape of the dome past point H is described by curve (c) in Figure 3-3. In both cases, the second derivatives are negative. To have a maximum value, therefore, the second derivative has to be negative.

Consider point L. The shape of the bowl prior to point L is described by curve (a) in Figure 3-2, while the shape of the bowl past point L is described by curve (a) in Figure 3-3. In both cases, the second derivatives are positive. To have a minimum value, therefore, the second derivative has to be positive.

Optimization in Algebra

The first-order condition for either a maximum or a minimum is that the first derivative is zero:

$$y' = 0 \qquad\qquad (3\text{-}49)$$

The first-order condition gives us an optimal value that can be either a maximum or a minimum. To determine that the optimal value is one or the other, we take the second derivative. If the second derivative is negative, the optimal value is a maximum; and if the second derivative is positive, the optimal value is a minimum:

$$y'' < 0 \text{ for a maximum} \qquad\qquad (3\text{-}50)$$
$$y'' > 0 \text{ for a minimum} \qquad\qquad (3\text{-}51)$$

Example One

Given demand and total cost functions

$$P = 1500 - 3Q \qquad\qquad (3\text{-}52)$$
$$TC = 45,000 + 300Q + 2Q^2 \qquad (3\text{-}53)$$

we want to determine the quantity of output that maximizes profits.

According to (3-21), the profit function is

$$\pi = TR(Q) - TC(Q) \qquad (3\text{-}21)$$

Since $TR(Q) = P \times Q$, and $P = 1{,}500 - 3Q$,
$$TR(Q) = 1{,}500Q - 3Q^2 \qquad (3\text{-}54)$$

From (3-54) and (3-53)

$$
\begin{aligned}
\pi &= TR(Q) - TC(Q) \\
&= 1{,}500Q - 3Q^2 - (45{,}000 + 300Q + 2Q^2) \\
&= -5Q^2 + 1{,}200Q - 45{,}000 \qquad (3\text{-}55)
\end{aligned}
$$

Taking the derivative of π with respect to Q in (3-55) and setting the derivative equal to zero,

$$d\pi/dQ = -10Q + 1{,}200 = 0 \qquad (3\text{-}56)$$

Solving for Q

$$
\begin{aligned}
10Q &= 1{,}200 \\
Q &= 120 \qquad (3\text{-}57)
\end{aligned}
$$

The optimal quantity is 120 units. To make sure that profits are maximized at $Q = 120$, we take the second derivative of (3-55) or another first derivative of (3-56):

$$d^2\pi/dQ^2 = -10 < 0 \qquad (3\text{-}58)$$

Since the second derivative is negative, profits at $Q = 120$ are maximized, not minimized. The second-order condition is met. The actual profit is obtained by plugging $Q = 120$ into equation (3-55).

Example Two

Given total revenue and total cost functions, $TR = f(Q)$ and $TC = f(Q)$, we would like to determine conditions for profit maximization.

Algebraic operations for this problem have already been introduced. From profit function (3-21)

$$\pi = TR(Q) - TC(Q) \qquad (3\text{-}21)$$

The first derivative of the profit function is

$$d\pi/dQ = MR(Q) - MC(Q) \qquad (3\text{-}23)$$

The second derivative is

$$d^2\pi/dQ^2 = MR'(Q) - MC'(Q) \qquad (3\text{-}40)$$

To derive the first-order condition, we set the first derivative in (3-23) equal to zero:

$$d\pi/dQ = MR(Q) - MC(Q) = 0 \qquad (3\text{-}59)$$

The first order condition is

$$MR(Q) = MC(Q), \qquad (3\text{-}60)$$

which is the familiar MR = MC rule for profit maximization. The second-order condition is obtained by setting the second derivative (3-40) at less than zero:

$$d^2\pi/dQ^2 = MR'(Q) - MC'(Q) < 0 \qquad (3\text{-}61)$$

The second order condition is

$$MR'(Q) < MC'(Q), \qquad (3\text{-}62)$$

which means that the slope of the marginal revenue curve should be smaller than the slope of the marginal cost curve.

Summary

Decision making that involves solutions of maximization and minimization problems is called optimization. Business decision-making is an optimization process. The first derivative of total function is the marginal function of the total function and measures the slope of the total function or the rate of change of the total function. The first derivative of total cost function, for instance, is the marginal cost function.

The rules of differentiation, reviewed in this chapter, are the following. The derivative of a constant is zero, while the derivative of a power function is obtained by moving the power of the independent variable to the front and subtracting 1 from the power. The derivative of a sum (or a difference) of two or more functions is the sum (or difference) of their separate derivatives. The derivative of the product of two functions is equal to the first function times the derivative of the second function, plus the second function times the derivative of the first function. The derivative of the quotient of two functions is equal to the denominator times the derivative of the numerator, minus the numerator times the derivative of the denominator, all divided by the denominator squared.

The second derivative is the derivative of a derivative, and measures the slope, or the rate of change of the first derivative. When a function has more than one independent variable, partial derivatives are taken with respect to each of the independent variables. Partial derivatives measure the change in the dependent variable in response to changes in one of the independent variables with all other independent variables remaining constant at fixed values.

There are two conditions for optimization. The first-order condition for either a maximum or a minimum is that the first derivative is zero, while the second-order condition is that the second derivative is negative for a maximum and positive for a minimum.

Endnotes

1.   Note that we assume all functions are continuous and smooth so that these functions are differentiable.

Chapter 4

Regression Analysis: Hypothesis Testing

Let us pose a hypothesis that study hours are important in determining a student's grade. If the hypothesis were not true, students would be wise to search for ways other than studying longer hours if they want to improve their grades. In reality, we may not know for sure whether study hours are, in fact, important in determining grades until we test the hypothesis empirically.

When a regression equation carries only one independent variable, the equation is called a **simple regression**. When a regression is based on a probable hypothesis, it is called a **model**. Our grade determining hypothesis may be expressed as the following linear regression model:

$$Y = a + bX + e \qquad (4\text{-}1)$$

where Y = grades measured in averages of test scores
X = weekly study hours.
Parameters, "a" and "b", are the intercept and the slope of the equation, and are called **regression coefficients**.

The last term "e" in equation (4-1) is known as the **random disturbance** or the **error term**. If we were to delete the error term from equation (4-1), the remaining algebraic relation between Y and X is so exact that changes in study hours should be interpreted as leading to directly proportionate changes in grades. An increase in study hours by one, for example, will raise the average score by "b", no more and no less. The addition of the error term indicates the statistical nature of the model in that the relation between grades and study hours as indicated in equation (4-1) is most likely neither exact nor applicable to all students.

Three reasons are normally cited for the use of the error term in a regression model. First, we may commit a **sampling error**: There is no guarantee that sample students we select are typical of the whole student body. Second, we may commit a **specification error**: We may have excluded from the model some important variables which we should have included, or have included in the model variables which we should have excluded. Third, we may commit a **measurement error** in reporting, copying, rounding, and other handling.

Once a model is specified, we need data to estimate the model. We may collect **time-series** data of grades and study hours of one or more students for the past several semesters, or collect **cross-sectional** data of grades and study hours of several students for one particular semester. We use sample data because it is either impossible or too costly to collect data of the population group which we may define as all students of our college.

Assumptions

Linear regression models are based on a number of assumptions:
(1) All the values of an independent variable should not be identical;
(2) The expected value of the error term is zero, i.e., $E(e) = 0$;
(3) The variance of the error term remains constant. That is $E(e)^2 = \sigma^2$ (read as sigma square);
(4) The values of the error term are not related to each other. That is, $E(e_i e_j) = 0$;
(5) In multiple regression analysis, one of the independent variables should not be a linear combination of any of the remaining independent variables; and
(6) The observations of the independent variable are considered fixed in   repeated samples and thus are independent of the error term.

Let us present an intuitive explanation of what would happen to regression analysis if any of these assumptions were violated.

If assumption (1) were not met, we would be unable to obtain estimates of the regression model. It is obvious that if the independent variable, study hours, remains identical at 10 hours for all sample students, there is no way of determining how changes in study hours would affect test scores.

In assumption (2), the symbol E stands for the **expected value** which may be defined as the mean of a probability distribution. Given random ten numbers, for instance, the expected value of these numbers is the arithmetic average of the ten numbers. To study the impact of the violation of assumption (2), let us review equation (4-1). In the equation, the constant term "a" represents the mean effect on Y of all excluded independent variables. Assuming that the expected value of "e" is a non-zero e', equation (4-1) may be restated as

$$Y = a + e' + bX. \qquad (4-2)$$

The violation of assumption (2) is seen in equation (4-2) to change the constant term from "a" to (a + e'), but leave the "b" coefficient unbiased.

Since the constant term carries no operational interpretation to start with in most regression models, we do not worry about the violation of assumption (2). This also explains why our analysis in this chapter is limited to the slope estimator "b", ignoring the intercept estimator "a". Furthermore, the assumption of zero expected error cannot be tested empirically since the ordinary least squares estimators generate residuals, empirical counterpart of the error term, whose mean is zero.

Variance measures why widely scattered around the differences are between actual values of the dependent variable and the values of the dependent variable that the regression model predicts. When assumption (3) is violated, the variance of the error term does not remain constant and we have a problem called **heteroscedasticity**. Heteroscedasticity could be a problem in time-series data, if underlying conditions that generated the data had been changed during the period that the data were collected. It is more common in cross section data that may contain two or more distinctive subgroups in such terms as income, region, industry, and others. The primary effect of heteroscedasticity is not on the biasedness of estimated coefficients but on larger standard errors of coefficients that lower t- values for the coefficients.

The violations of assumptions (4) and (5) are known as autocorrelation and multicollinearity, respectively. Autocorrelation and multicollinearity are discussed in detail in the next chapter.

Assumption (6) tells us that if we were to collect Y observations again with the same values of the same independent variables, we should be able to obtain the same Y observations as before. The ability to repeat Y observations with the same values of the same independent variables depends upon two conditions. One condition relates to no errors in measurement. The errors in measurement , if existed, are known as the errors in variables problem and are limited to independent variables since errors in measurement of the dependent variable are one of the reasons for adding the error term to the regression model. Since there is no formal way of testing whether or not the errors in measurement of independent variables exist, we may simply point out that theory underlying the model and knowledge of the way in which the data are collected are the best way by which the errors in measurement problem can be examined and, hopefully, avoided. The other condition is the absence of simultaneous interaction among independent variables. Put differently, independent variables should not depend on one another.

Estimation

Suppose that we collected data for a five-student sample in order to estimate the model specified as (4-1). In Table 4-1, the first student studied 4 hours a week and scored 60 points, while the remaining four students studied 8, 8, 9, and 11 hours per week and scored 70, 80, 80, and 90 points respectively.

These observations are plugged into standard regression softwares, and the estimates are summarized in equation 4-3.

$$Y = 42.1539 + 4.2308 \ X \qquad (4\text{-}3)$$
$$(0.8368)$$
$$R^2 = 0.8950$$
$$D\text{-}W = 3.0939$$

Table 4-1. Data for the Test Score Model

Student Number	Test Scores	Weekly Study Hours
1	60	4
2	70	8
3	80	8
4	80	9
5	90	11

In equation (4-3), the estimated value of "a" in equation (4-1) is 42.1539 and the estimated value of "b" is 4.2308. The value (0.8368) printed below the estimated "b" is called the standard error of the estimated coefficient. R^2 is called the coefficient of determination and D-W is an abbreviation of the Durbin-Watson statistic.

Before we go over these statistics, consider what the equation is trying to tell us. According to equation (4-3), if a student does not study at all so that $X = 0$, the test score (Y) is expected to be 42.1539 points, since

$$Y = 42.1539 + 4.2308 \ (0)$$
$$= 42.1539. \qquad (4\text{-}4)$$

For every additional hour that a student spends on studying, the test score is expected to increase by 4.2308 points, which is the slope coefficient. The big question is: Are these numbers and interpretations reliable? The remainder of this chapter and the next are designed to answer the question.

It may be reminded that data do not always look as reasonable as they are shown in Table 4-1. Sometimes, data points are obviously too large or too small relative to the rest of the data. These abnormal observations are called **outliers**. Outliers may result from the errors of measurement or from some special events. The presence of outliers in the data, if not corrected, increases errors in estimated coefficients. If there are only one or two outliers and they are measurement errors, they may be adjusted to the mean of a few data points observed under similar conditions. If outliers are the results of some special events, dummy variables may be used to account for outliers. Dummy variables are explained in Chapter 5.

Test of Hypothesis

Regression models enable us to test a causal relation between the dependent and the independent variables. The causal relation is usually stated in the form of a hypothesis or a null hypothesis. In the grade determining model, the null hypothesis is that the number of study hours is *not* a significant determinant of a student's grade. To test the hypothesis, we developed a simple regression model in (4-2), collected data, and estimated the model using the ordinary least squares (OLS) method. The "b" coefficient was found to be 4.2308 in the estimated model. We need to determine whether we should accept or reject the null hypothesis based on the estimates.

Review of Concepts

Given a simple regression model

$$Y = a + bX + e \qquad (4-1)$$

the hypothesis implied in the model is that X is a **statistically significant** determinant of Y, meaning that the relation between X and Y as indicated in "b" cannot be explained by sampling errors or a chance factor alone. If the value of "b" were zero, it is clear that changes in X would have no impact on Y. The zero value of "b", i.e., b = 0, is called the **null hypothesis**, and our objective in regression analysis is to find out whether we should accept or reject the null hypothesis.

When we make the decision of accepting or rejecting a hypothesis, we are faced with two kinds of errors. **Type I error** is committed when we reject a hypothesis which is in fact true, and **Type II error** is committed when we accept a hypothesis which is in fact false. The two types of errors depend on each other in that when we try to reduce the probability of rejecting the true hypothesis, we will be increasing the probability of accepting the false hypothesis. The normal procedure, therefore, is to pre-select and hold constant the probability of committing Type I error and then to minimize the probability of committing Type II error.

The probability level of committing Type I error, i.e., of rejecting a true hypothesis, is known as α (read as alpha), or the **level of significance**. The α level, selected most often in regression analysis, is 0.05 or 5 percent. One may also use 0.01 or 0.10, but none greater than 0.10. Unless stated otherwise, we use 0.05 as our pre-selected α level. The only way to lower both types of errors is to increase the sample size. Once the sample size reaches the total population, Type I and Type II errors will cease to exist.

When models are estimated with small samples with no knowledge on the population mean and the population standard deviation, we use the so-called t-distribution instead of the normal distribution. In the normal distribution, the mean plus and minus one, two, and 1.96 standard deviations under a normal curve encompasses 68.26%, 95.45%, and 95%, respectively. The t- distribution is flatter than the normal distribution although the extent of flatness of the t-distribution depends on the degrees of freedom.

The number of the **degrees of freedom** refers to the difference between the number of randomly selected observations and the number of constraints placed on the observations. The degrees of freedom, or d.f., in regression models are defined as the number of observations (n) minus the number of parameters (m) to be estimated in the model.

Unless regression models are estimated in deviations from the mean, the number of parameters equals the total number of variables in the model. In our grade determining model, for instance, n = 5 and m = 2 for one dependent and one independent variables, so that the number of degrees of freedom is 3. When the number of degrees of freedom reaches 30 or more, there is little difference between the t-distribution and the normal distribution. Since we have to use the t-distribution for small samples (n ≥ 30) and since there is little difference between the two distributions for large samples, we simply use the t-distribution in regression analysis.

Returning to estimated equation (4-3), if the estimated coefficient is statistically significant, we reject the null hypothesis and conclude that the number of study hours is a significant determinant of a student's grade. If the estimated coefficient is not significant statistically, we accept the null hypothesis and conclude that, based on our data, the number of study hours cannot be said a significant determinant of a student's grade. We use t-test to decide whether or not the estimated coefficient is statistically significant.

t-Test

We illustrate the t-test by use of our grade determining model (4-3). The estimated value of "b" is 4.2308. The null hypothesis that we wish to test is that study hours have no impact on test scores, that is, b = 0. Please remember that the true value of "b" is unknown and most likely we will never know what the true value is. We simply try to have a good idea of what the true value is by *inferring* from the estimated value of "b" in equation (4-3). The process of doing so is thus called a **statistical inference**.

In order to test whether the estimated value of "b" is significantly different from zero, we need to know the standard error, s_b, of "b". The s_b is the standard deviation of the "b" estimate which is obtained, in theory, from repeated samples. The s_b is called the **standard error of estimated b coefficient**. The estimated value of s_b in (4-3) is 0.8368. To perform a t-test, we need to find a t-value for the estimated coefficient of "b", which is obtained as

$$t_b = b/s_b \qquad\qquad (4\text{-}5)$$

In equation (4-2), the t-value for the estimated coefficient of b is

$$t_b = 4.2308/0.8368 = 5.0559. \qquad (4\text{-}6)$$

Usually, regression softwares provide the t-values concurrently with the values of other estimates.

Does this "t" value tell us to reject the null hypothesis or accept the null hypothesis? To answer this question we need to perform a t-test under the t-distribution. In t-test, we compare the t-value for the estimated coefficient (t_b) with the reference t value, which we denote as t_α, read from the t-table presented at the end of this book. The reference t-value is one for a pre-selected α level and the number of degrees of freedom appropriate for a given model. In (4-3), the α level is pre-selected at 5 percent (i.e., 0.05) and the number of degrees of freedom is 3. The reference t value for our estimated "b" is indicated as 3.182 in the t-table, crossed vertically by $\alpha = 0.05$ and d.f. = 3.

The actual test is to compare the two t values. If $t_b > t_\alpha$, the estimated value of b is statistically significant. If $t_b < t_\alpha$, the estimated value of "b" is statistically insignificant. The term "statistically significant" means that the estimated value of "b" is significantly different from zero. Since the estimated value of "b" is not zero, the estimated value is said to be statistically significant.

In the grade determining model, the t_b is 5.0559 and is greater than $t_\alpha = 3.182$. We thus reject the null hypothesis and conclude that study hours are a significant determinant of a student's test scores. Alternatively, we may state that the estimated value of "b" is statistically significant at 5 percent level.

Once the estimated value of "b" is found statistically significant, we interpret the estimated coefficient (4.2308) in such a way that the relation between the dependent and the independent variable as indicated by the estimated coefficient is exact by saying that an increase in weekly study hours by one hour will lead to an increase in test scores by 4.2308 points. The estimated value of "b" is called the **point estimate** in contrast to confidence interval estimates which we will study in the next section.

Confidence Interval Estimation

The true meaning of the t-test can be easily understood when confidence intervals are estimated for the same estimated coefficient. The formula for the **confidence interval estimation** is:

$$\hat{b} - t_\alpha(s_b) < b < \hat{b} + t_\alpha(s_b) \qquad (4\text{-}7)$$

where $\hat{b}$ = estimated "b" coefficient
t_α = t-value at a given level of α
s_b = standard error of the estimated "b".

By plugging all appropriate values from the grade determining model into (4-6), we obtain:

$$[4.2308\text{-}(3.182\text{x}0.8368)] < b < [4.2308 + (3.182\text{x}0.8368] \qquad (4\text{-}8)$$
$$1.5681 < b < 6.8935 \qquad (4\text{-}9)$$

What do these two figures mean?

Our grade determining model has been estimated with the sample of only five students. If we select five student samples at random 100 times while maintaining the values of the independent variable constant, estimate the same model 100 times with these 100 different five student samples, and compute confidence intervals 100 times, 95 (= 1 - 0.05) of these 100 confidence intervals will then include the true parameter "b" for the whole student body which is an unknown, unique value that does not change.

In reality, we interpret as if our interval of 1.5681 to 6.8935 is one of the 95 intervals that contain the true value of "b" by saying that we are 95 percent confident that the true "b" lies between the **lower limit**

1.5681 and the **upper limit** 6.8935. Further, when the estimated confidence interval does not contain zero between the two limits, the estimated "b" coefficient is statistically significant, meaning that both the t test and the confidence interval test result in the identical significance test of "b".

If we lower the confidence level by selecting a larger α, the interval between the lower limit (1.5681) and the upper limit (6.8935) would be narrower. The t-value at $\alpha = .20$ with 3 degrees of freedom, for instance, is 1.638. Recomputing the confidence interval with this smaller t-value, we obtain:

$$[4.2308-(1.638 \times 0.8368)] < b < [4.2308+(1.638 \times 0.8368)] \quad (4\text{-}10)$$
$$2.8601 < b < 5.6015 \quad (4\text{-}11)$$

The confidence interval was narrowed from (1.5681 to 6.8935) to (2.8601 to 5.6015) as we lowered the confidence level from 95 to 80 percent. It is intuitively clear that the intervals will have to be $-\infty$ to $+\infty$ for us to be 100 percent confident.

It is customary to compute the confidence level at the 95, 99, or, at the lowest, 90 percent level. This corresponds to our earlier statement that the pre-selected α should be 0.05, 0.01, or at the most 0.10.

R^2

R^2, called the **coefficient of determination** or the R square, tells us the percentage of variation of the dependent variable that is explained by the regression model. In (4-2), study hours explain 89.5 percent of variation of test scores.

At least in principle, the value of R^2 ranges from zero, meaning that the model is totally irrelevant, to one, indicating that the model is perfect. In reality, R^2 is less than one because the value of one most likely indicates that the model is an identity that requires no estimation. The value is greater than zero because even a totally irrelevant independent variable will have some bearing on the dependent variable since we are dealing with numbers. This also means that, *ceteris paribus*, the value of R^2 tends to be greater as the number of independent variables increases. A good regression model does not include many variables, however. When a model attains its optimal performance, inclusion of additional variables adds little, if any, to accuracy. If two models yield the same accuracy, the one that contains fewer variables should be chosen. This is the **principle of parsimony**.

Summary

Through regression, we test hypothesis. A regression model has an error term that disappears upon estimation. Three reasons for adding an error term in regression are sampling error, specification error, and measurement error. A regression model is estimated using time-series or cross-section data. Once a regression model is estimated, the estimated values of all coefficients, standard errors of estimated coefficients, the coefficient of determination and the Durbin-Watson statistic are presented. Before the estimated coefficients are interpreted, a t-test has to be performed and the problems of multicollinearity and autocorrelation have to be evaluated.

To perform a t-test, the level of significance has to be preselected normally at 1, 5, or 10 percent level, and the number of degrees of freedom has to be obtained by subtracting the number of parameters to be estimated from the number of observations. In t-test, we compare the t-value for the estimated coefficient with the reference t value, read from the t-table for a pre-selected α level and the number of degrees of freedom. The t-value for the estimated coefficient has to be greater than the reference t-value for the estimated coefficient to be statistically significant. Only after the estimated coefficient is found significant, we may interpret the estimated coefficient. The estimated coefficient is called the point estimate in contrast to confidence interval estimates. Confidence intervals are associated with a $(1 - \alpha)$ level of confidence. R^2, called the coefficient of determination, measures the percentage of variation of the dependent variable that is explained by the regression model.

Chapter 5

Regression Analysis: Additional Properties

Test of a regression model starts from the significance test of estimated coefficients, discussed in Chapter 4. There are several additional concepts that we need to know in order for us to apply regression analysis to actual business and economic problems. We begin from test of two assumptions that, like t-test, require a routine evaluation before estimates of a regression model are interpreted. Problems arising from violation of the two assumptions are called multicollinearity and autocorrelation.

Multicollinearity

It is rare that regression models contain only one independent variable. The problems we often encounter are more likely how many independent variables to include in the model and which ones to exclude from it. One of the assumptions listed early in Chapter 4 is that one of the independent variables in a multiple regression model should not be a linear combination of any of the remaining independent variables. Violation of this assumption causes a multicollinearity problem.

What It Is and How It Affects

When data of two or more independent variables move closely together in a linear relationship, these variables are said collinear. When the collinearity among independent variables is serious enough to affect our regression estimates, a **multicollinearity** problem is said to exist. The problem of multicollinearity is not its existence, but the degree of its severity, since statistical observations of independent variables will not be completely independent of one another.

The cause of multicollinearity is a trend common to some of the independent variables. In developing a forecasting model of a company's sales, for instance, we may include income and price index variables in the model as independent variables. If we use nominal or money income instead of real income, we are likely to face a multicollinearity problem since inflation affects both money income and the price index.

A dramatic example of the multicollinearity problem is to see how a perfect collinearity affects the estimation of regression coefficients. Perfect collinearity exists when, for example, the observations of one independent variable are 1, 2 and 3, while the observations of another independent variable are 2, 4, and 6. If we happen to plug observations that are perfectly collinear into the computer for regression estimation, the computer will give us a message to the effect of a **singular matrix** or a **matrix singularity**. Matrix singularity means that the computer cannot compute regression coefficients because matrices representing the denominators of least squares estimators possess no inverse which is needed to complete the computation.

Multicollinearity that we face in practical regression studies is less severe, but more difficult to deal with. The major impact of multicollinearity would be on standard errors of estimated regression coefficients. This is because the formulas for estimating the variances of the estimated coefficients contain the correlation between independent variables in the denominator with a negative sign. This means that a high correlation between two collinear independent variables will cause high variances and thus large standard errors of estimated coefficients.

Although the presence of multicollinearity leaves least squares estimators unbiased and the R^2 statistic unaffected, large standard errors of estimated coefficients will increase the possibility of accepting the null hypothesis, and of obtaining a wider confidence interval even if the null hypothesis were rejected. When a regression model is affected by a serious multicollinearity problem, it is not unusual to experience a high R^2 while many of estimated coefficients are statistically insignificant.

How to Find

A couple of methods are available for test of the multicollinearity problem. The first is to check the simple correlation coefficient matrix of the data set and see whether the correlation coefficient between any two independent variables is as high as, say, 0.9 or greater. If the correlation coefficient between two independent variables is high and if one or both estimated coefficients of these variables are not significant, the presence of multicollinearity becomes a suspect.

The second method of testing the presence of multicollinearity is to see how existing coefficients and their standard errors of a particular model change as we add a new independent variable to the model. In practice, we may estimate the model twice, once by dropping one of two variables suspected of multicollinearity from the model and the second time by adding both variables in the model. We then compare estimated coefficients and their standard errors. We may also use the stepwise regression method to test changes in regression coefficients and their standard errors.

The most common **stepwise regression** method instructs the computer to add independent variables one by one in order of the contribution that these variables make to the R^2 statistic. At each step, the computer prints all major statistics including estimated coefficients and standard errors. We can test the presence of multicollinearity by checking whether existing coefficients and standard errors have changed substantially as new independent variables are added.

What to Do

Once the presence of a multicollinearity has been confirmed, we should take a step or two to alleviate the problem. First, if the collinearity between any two independent variables appears to be extremely high, one of the two variables may have to be dropped. This solution depends on how important the variable is which we consider dropping. If the true parameter of the variable is not zero as is the case with a price variable in a demand function, we may be committing a specification error by dropping the price variable and end up with biased coefficients for the remaining variables. Second, we may not do anything to correct the problem if the model is intended for forecasting and the multicollinearity among included independent variables is expected to prevail throughout the forecasting period. We may also do nothing, if estimated coefficients of independent variables involved in multicollinearity are statistically significant.

Autocorrelation

When the error term is correlated with its own past values, an **autocorrelation** or a **serial correlation** is said to exist. Autocorrelation occurs normally in time series data.

What Causes It

The cause of autocorrelation is a **misspecification** of the model. The misspecification is of two types; omission of relevant variables and misspecification of the functional form. One example of the omission of relevant variables is to specify a quarterly sales forecasting model without including a variable that represents quarterly variations in sales.

Misspecification of the functional form occurs when we try to fit linear models to phenomena that are essentially nonlinear. One example relates to long run average cost curves of firms that are presented as U-shaped. If we try to apply linear models for estimation of these nonlinear cost functions, it is probable that autocorrelation would be a problem in these models. Misspecification of the functional form may also occur if we try to fit linear models to observations that are growing at an increasing rate.

How to Find

The most widely accepted way of testing whether or not a regression model exhibits a serious autocorrelation is to use the **Durbin-Watson (D-W) statistic.** [1]

The cookbook procedure of the D-W test is as follows. In the Durbin-

Watson statistic table printed at the end of this book, we find lower (d_L) and upper (d_U) critical values for the D-W statistic, crossed vertically by the number of observations (n) and horizontally by the number of independent variables (k'). For observations smaller than 15, we read critical values for n = 15, while for observations larger than 100, we use the row for n = 100. The number of observations and the number of independent variables for our grade determining model in (4-3) are respectively 5 and 1, and the relevant critical values are d_L = 0.95 and d_U = 1.23.

We draw a line that shows zero at the left end, 2 at the midpoint, and 4 at the right end, as indicated in Figure 5-1. We indicate d_L and d_U values to the left of the midpoint and (4-d_U) and (4-d_L) to the right of the midpoint. If the D-W statistic of a particular regression belongs to the two outside ranges [i.e., 0 to d_L and (4 - d_L) to 4], there exists a serious autocorrelation in the regression. If the D-W statistic belongs to the two intermediate areas [i.e., d_L to d_U and (4 - d_U) to (4 - d_L)], there may or may not be an autocorrelation problem. If the D-W statistic belongs to the middle area [i.e. d_U to (4 - d_U)], the model is safe from the autocorrelation problem.

The D-W statistic for our model is 3.09 in equation (4-3), which belongs to the autocorrelation area since 3.09 is greater than 3.05 (= 4 - 0.95).

```
0                    2                  4
|------|------|------|------|------|-------|
   d_L     d_U         (4-d_U) (4-d_L)
```

Figure 5-1 Durbin-Watson Test. If a D-W statistic falls between d_U and (4 - d_U), the test indicates that the model is safe from autocorrelation. If a D-W statistic falls between d_L and d_U or between (4 - d_U) and (4 - d_L), the test is inconclusive. If a D-W statistic belongs to the two outlying areas, the model suffers autocorrelation.

What to Do

If the D-W statistic of a regression model belongs to the safe area, we simply state that autocorrelation is not a problem in the model and do nothing. If the D-W statistic belongs to the inconclusive or indeterminate areas, we normally state that it belongs to the inconclusive area and do nothing. Sometimes, when the D-W statistic tilts close to the problem areas, we may attempt to correct the autocorrelation problem as if the D-W statistic belongs to the two problem areas.

In essence, there are two ways of correcting the problem. One relates to changing the model specification, and the other, to purely statistical adjustments. Changing the model specification means either to find and add omitted variables which should have been included in the model, or to modify the functional form so that the model can adequately represent actual observations. Correcting the autocorrelation problem through changes in the model specification is preferable to purely statistical adjustments, of which the most popular one is the Cochrane-Orcutt (C-O) adjustment.[2]

Dummy Variables

One of the prerequisites to developing a successful econometric model is that the variables are quantifiable so that we can collect data for these variables. Sometimes, variables we wish to include in the model represent qualitative differences and are called **dummy variables**. Examples include gender status, war or peace, race, quarterly or seasonal fluctuations, and different regions. Dummy variables are encountered mostly in the independent variables, although dummy variables can also be used as the dependent variable. Other names of dummy variables are **qualitative, categorical,** or **binary variables.**

Estimation

To illustrate how a dummy variable is utilized in regression models, we add another column to Table 4-1. The last column in Table 5-1 is a dummy variable in which female = 1 and male = 0.

Table 5-1. Data with the Dummy Variable

Student	Test Scores	Weekly Study Hours	Female = 1 Male = 0
1	60	4	0
2	70	8	1
3	80	8	0
4	80	9	1
5	90	11	1

Estimates of the expanded model are shown in equation (5-1). Estimates of the model with the dummy variable, summarized in (5-1), may be compared with estimates of the original model (4-3) without the dummy variable, reprinted as (5-2). The dummy variable picks up some of impact captured by the constant term, which is smaller in (5-1). With additional variables, the value of R^2 is increased.

$$Y = 36.8421 + 5.5263X - 8.4210D \qquad (5\text{-}1)$$
$$(0.7207) \quad (3.3547)$$
$$R^2 = 0.99$$

where Y = test scores
      X = study hours
      D = dummy variable for gender; 1 for female and 0 for male.

$$Y = 42.1539 + 4.2308X \qquad\qquad (5\text{-}2)$$
$$(0.8368)$$
$$R^2 = 0.895$$

Assuming that the estimated coefficient for the dummy variable is statistically significant, the impact of the dummy variable is to shift the intercept of the estimated equation. In equation (5-1), the estimated equation for female students is

$$Y = 36.8421 + 5.5263X - 8.4210(1)$$
$$= 28.4211 + 5.5263X \qquad (5\text{-}3)$$

The same equation for male students is

$$Y = 36.8421 + 5.5263X - 8.4210(0)$$
$$Y = 36.8421 + 5.5263X \qquad (5\text{-}4)$$

One alternative to the use of dummy variables is to estimate two separate equations for male and female. The major disadvantage of this alternative is the loss in the number of the degrees of freedom. In our grade determining model, for instance, the separate estimation implies a zero degree of freedom for male equation since we have only two male students in our five student sample, and one degree of freedom for female students. The dummy variable has an advantage of preserving a larger number of the degrees of freedom when qualitative variables are present in an regression model.

Proper Use of a Dummy Variable

One may note that we had only one dummy variable, D, for two gender categories, male and female. Assume that we include two dummy variables, one for each gender, as follows:

$$Y = a + bX + cF + dM \qquad (5\text{-}5)$$

where F = dummy for female students
      D = dummy for male students

Equation (5-5), then, suffers from the so-called *linearly dependent* relation between the two dummy variables F and M, which creates a perfect multicollinearity and makes it impossible to estimate the regression parameters because of the matrix singularity. As a rule, we always subtract one from the options represented by the dummy variable.

To further illustrate the proper use of dummy variables, let us develop a quarterly deposit forecasting model of a commercial bank.

$$DDT = a + b_1Y + b_2RATE + b_3NOW + b_4Q_1$$
$$+ b_5Q_2 + b_6Q_3 + e \qquad (5\text{-}6)$$

where DDT = total demand deposit

RATE = market rate of interest

NOW = dummy variable for NOW account; 1 for periods prior to the beginning of NOW accounts and 0 for periods after the beginning of NOW accounts

Q_i = dummy variables for quarter i.

To avoid the matrix singularity, we dropped one of two dummy variables relating to the NOW account, and one of the four quarterly dummies. NOW (negotiable order of withdrawals) is a checking account that pays interest. In equation (5-6), we dropped the fourth quarter dummy, but it does not matter which one we drop so long as we drop one. The normal procedure is to drop a dummy with en estimated coefficient that is least significant.

Dummy Dependent Variables

Interesting applications of the dummy variable may be made when the dependent variable is represented by a dummy variable. Examples include the study of whether or not an individual will buy a new car, whether an individual will buy a domestic or a foreign car, whether a person will vote on a presidential election, and whether a student will fail on a particular test. We review one specific case to see how dummy variables can be used as the dependent variable.

Assume a group of doctors specializing in lung problems decide to find out the type of patients who are likely to develop a pulmonary disease. A patient is defined as a person who visits the doctor's office regardless of whether or not the person is later diagnosed to suffer from pulmonary disease. After reviewing files of all patients who have visited their office, the doctors may develop a regression model:

$$PLM = a + b_1Y + b_2A + b3H + b_4S + e \qquad (5\text{-}7)$$

where PLM = dummy for pulmonary disease; one if diagnosed to suffer a disease and zero otherwise

Y = income of the patient

A = age of the patient

H = dummy for hereditary factor; one if parents of the patient have had a pulmonary disease and zero otherwise

S = dummy for smoking; one for smokers and zero for patients who do not smoke.

The R^2 for equation (5-7) is not likely to be high because observations of the dependent variable are either one or zero. Still, estimates of the equation may be very interesting, since the predicted value of the dependent variable can be interpreted as the probability that a particular patient will have a pulmonary disease, given the patient's characteristics on income, age, hereditary factor, and smoking. Further, estimated coefficients reveal marginal contributions toward the probability, provided that other factors remain constant. For instance, smoking adds the value of b_4 to the probability that the smoking patient is likely to suffer a pulmonary disease.[3]

Nonlinear Regression

Functional relations in business, economics, and other subject areas to which regression methods are applied may not always be expressed in linear forms. Although our study of regression methods has so far been progressed in linear forms, it can easily be extended to deal with nonlinear functions.

Nonlinear Independent Variables

Algebraic functions with multi-terms are known as the **polynomial**

function which has the general form

$$Y = a + b_1X + b_2X^2 + \ldots + b_nX^n \qquad (5\text{-}8)$$

where the powers of the independent variables are nonnegative integers. The highest power involved is called the degree of the polynomial function. A cubic function, for example, is a third degree polynomial. Although total product and total cost curves are often depicted as a cubic function, it is rare that applied regression models go beyond the second degree polynomial:

$$Y = a + b_1X + b_2X^2 + e \qquad (5\text{-}9)$$

Any social phenomenon that exhibits a dome or a bowl shape may be approximated by this quadratic equation. A quadratic function will have a maximum value if the parameter of the squared term is negative, and a minimum value if the parameter is positive. This is because these signs are the signs of the second derivatives when expressed as an optimization problem.

Estimating a polynomial function is simple. Assume that we are interested in estimating a long-run average cost curve of a firm by specifying a second degree polynomial;

$$AC = a + b_1Q + b_2Q^2 + e \qquad (5\text{-}10)$$

where AC is the average cost and Q is the output. We collect data for AC and Q, and square Q to obtain observations of Q^2. We, then, estimate the average cost function as if it were a linear multiple regression model.

Logarithmic Transformation

When observations grow rather rapidly over time, one may experience an improvement in estimation by specifying the model in a multiplicative form instead of an additive form:

$$Y = f(X_1 X_2) \qquad (5\text{-}11)$$

By changing Y to Q, X_1 to L, and X_2 to K, and adding a constant term A, we obtain the Cobb-Douglas production function:

$$Q = AL^\alpha K^\beta \qquad (5\text{-}12)$$

where Q = output
L = labor
K = capital.

For simplicity, we dropped the disturbance term in (5-12).

The estimation of equation (5-12) requires its transformation to a *log* form:

$$ln\ Q = ln\ A + \alpha(ln\ L) + \beta(ln\ K) \quad (5\text{-}13)$$

Put differently, the estimation of equation (5-13) involves the collection of data for output, labor and capital, conversion of these data into natural logarithms, and a linear estimation of *ln* Q as a function of *ln* L and *ln* K. The symbol *ln* represents a natural logarithm.

Logarithms

There are two types of logarithms. When the base is 10, the logarithm is called **common logarithm**, expressed as *log*, while the logarithm with the base "e" is known as **natural logarithm**, expressed as *ln*. Logarithms are used as a shortcut for a lengthy computation. Although common log and natural log are interchangeable, the common log is used mostly for algebraic computation whereas the natural log is used mostly for business and economic applications relating to the growth problem. Why is the natural log more convenient for business and economic applications?

Given a principal "P" and an interest rate "r", the future value F with annually **compound interest rate** would be

$$F = P(1 + r)^n \qquad (5\text{-}14)$$

where "n" is the number of years for the principal and the interest to stay untouched for compounding. Assuming that the interest is compounded "m" times a year, equation (5-14) changes to:

$$F = P(1 + r/m)^{mn}$$
$$= P[(1 + r/m)^{m/r}]^{rn} \qquad (5\text{-}15)$$

Let X stand for m/r. Equation (5-15) then becomes:

$$F = P[(1 + 1/X)^{X}]^{rn} \qquad (5\text{-}16)$$

As X approaches infinity, the term within the large bracket approaches a limit and becomes the number "e":

$$\lim_{X \to \infty} (1 + 1/X)^{X} = e \approx 2.7183 \qquad (5\text{-}17)$$

Put differently, the limiting value of $(1 + 1/X)^{X}$ as X increases to infinity would be 2.7183 to four places after the decimal. Equation (5-16) now becomes

$$F = Pe^{rn}, \qquad (5\text{-}18)$$

which can be solved by use of the natural log.

The number "e" may be interpreted as the value of one dollar at the end of one year, when the dollar is invested at an annual interest rate of 100 percent with continuous compounding. See the illustration in Table 5-2 of a compound interest with a beginning principal of one dollar and the annual interest of 100 percent. No matter how many times the interest may be compounded, the amount of principal plus interest at the end of the year will never reach $2.719. It is the continuously compounding nature of "e" which makes it so appealing to economic applications since many economic variables grow also at a continuously compounding rate.

Table 5-2. Compound Interest and Natural Value

Number of times that interest is compounded during a year	Principal plus interest at the end of the year
1	$2.00
2	2.25
5	2.49
10	2.59
100	2.70
1000	2.717
10000	2.718

Summary

Before regression coefficients are interpreted, the problems of multicollinearity and autocorrelation have to be evaluated along with the t-test.

When data of two or more independent variables move together in a linear relationship closely enough to affect our regression estimates, a multicollinearity problem is said to exist. The cause of multicollinearity is a trend common to some of the independent variables such as inflation in a forecasting model. If the computer cannot compute coefficients because of severe multicollinearity, matrix singularity is indicated. The presence of multicollinearity leaves least squares estimators unbiased and the R^2 statistic unaffected, but large standard errors of estimated coefficients lead to lower t-values and thus increase the possibility of accepting the null hypothesis. Once the presence of a multicollinearity has been confirmed, we may drop one of two variables involved in multicollinearity, or do nothing if estimated coefficients of independent variables involved in multicollinearity are statistically significant.

When the error term is correlated with its own past values, there is an autocorrelation. Autocorrelation is caused by a misspecification of the model either through omission of relevant variables or through misspecification of the functional form. The presence of autocorrelation is tested by the Durbin-Watson test. If a D-W statistic falls between d_U and $(4 - d_U)$, the model is safe from autocorrelation. If a D-W statistic falls between d_L and d_U or between $(4 - d_U)$ and $(4 - d_L)$, the test is inconclusive. If a D-W statistic belongs to the two outlying areas, the model suffers autocorrelation. Autocorrelation may be corrected by respecifying the model or the Cochrane-Orcutt adjustment.

Regression models may be improved by use of dummy variables that represent qualitative differences such as months, four seasons, or regional differences. The dummy variable has an advantage of preserving a larger number of the degrees of freedom. The proper use of the dummy variable is to subtract one from the options represented by the dummy variable. A dummy variable may also be used as the dependent variable. In this case the dummy variable may indicate the probability that the particular event represented by the dummy variable is materialized.

Finally, a multiplicative function with powers is estimated by taking natural logarithms of the function.

Endnotes

1.   J. Durbin and G. S. Watson, "Testing for Serial Correlation in Least Squares Regression," *Biometrika*, 38 (1951), 159-177.

2.   D. Cochrane and G. H. Orcutt, "Application of Least Squares Regression to Relationships Containing Autocorrelated Error Terms," *Journal of the American Statistical Association*, 44 (1949), 32-61.

3.   Two problems may arise when the dependent variable is represented by a dummy variable. One is the possibility that the estimated probabilities may lie outside the 0-1 range. This problem may be corrected by either the probit or the logit model, both of which involve a cumbersome computation. The other problem is that the variance of the error term varies with the

dependent variable, resulting in the variance of the regression coefficient which may no longer be the minimum.

Chapter 6

Demand Elasticities

Firms produce products and sell them to make profits. To generate the maximum profit, owners of all businesses try to be careful in selecting the prices of their products. As a first step toward selecting the maximum-profit price, the owner may want to know how changes in price affect the firm's sales. The owner would not want to lower the price below the wholesale price, since a price below cost means a loss to her. The owner would not want to raise the price too high either, since the quantity of sales may be too small to make profits at higher prices. Information on how responsive sales are to price changes would be beneficial to the store owner in selecting an optimal sales price, especially during holidays or other times when the store has excess inventory.

The Price Elasticity of Demand

The **price elasticity of demand** is an indicator of buyers' response, in terms of changes in the quantity demanded, to changes in the price of a good or service. The price elasticity is measured by the ratio of the percentage change in the quantity of a good or service demanded to the percentage change in the price of the good or service.

Defining the Price Elasticity

The price elasticity of demand E_p is defined as

$$E_p = \frac{\text{percentage change in quantity demanded}}{\text{percentage change in price}} \qquad (6\text{-}1)$$

Using symbols,

$$E_p = [\frac{\Delta Q}{Q} \times 100] \div [\frac{\Delta P}{P} \times 100] \qquad (6\text{-}2)$$

In (6-2), the sign "Δ" indicates a change and the figure "100" converts numbers into percentage terms. Since both the numerator and the denominator contain 100, (6-2) can be simplified:

$$\begin{aligned} E_p &= (\Delta Q/Q) \div (\Delta P/P) \\ &= (\Delta Q/Q) \times (P/\Delta P) \\ &= (\Delta Q/\Delta P) \times (P/Q) \qquad (6\text{-}3) \end{aligned}$$

Taking the limit of E_p in (6-3)

$$\lim_{\Delta P \to 0} E_p = \frac{dQ}{dP} \times \frac{P}{Q} \qquad (6\text{-}4)$$

We use (6-4) to estimate elasticity coefficients.

Price Elasticity in Linear Demand Functions

Expression (6-4) is quite convenient in estimating elasticities. Consider a linear demand function

$$Q = 100 - 2P \qquad (6\text{-}5)$$

The price elasticity of demand may be computed for different price levels. The price elasticity at $P = 10$, for instance, is

$$E_P = (dQ/dP) \times (P/Q)$$
$$= (-2) \times (10/80), \text{ since } Q = 80 \text{ at } P = 10 \text{ in (6-5)}$$
$$= -0.25 \qquad (6\text{-}6)$$

The price elasticity at $P = 20$ is

$$E_P = (-2) \times (20/60)$$
$$= -0.67 \qquad (6\text{-}7)$$

Interpreting the Elasticity Coefficient

Once the elasticity coefficient is computed, we need to know what the computed elasticity coefficient means. The sign of the elasticity coefficient is determined even before the elasticity coefficient is computed. The sign is negative when the two variables, price and quantity demanded, change in the opposite direction. The sign is positive when the two variables involved change in the same direction. The elasticity between price and quantity supplied is expected to have a positive sign because a higher price is associated with a larger quantity supplied.

The elasticity coefficient -0.25 means that, at $P = 10$, as the price of the product changes by 1 percent, the quantity of the product demanded changes by 0.25 percent in the opposite direction. The elasticity coefficient -0.67 means that, at $P = 20$, as the price of the product changes by 1 percent, the quantity of the product demanded is expected to change by 0.67 percent in the opposite direction.

Classifying the Price Elasticity

The concept of price elasticity of demand can be applied to a wide range of goods and services, even though no elasticity coefficients are actually computed. To use the elasticity concept for decision-making purposes, we need to classify the elasticity coefficients into five categories: completely elastic, relatively elastic, unitary elastic, relatively inelastic, and completely inelastic. Since the sign itself has no bearing on determining whether the demand for a given good or service is elastic or inelastic, the classification of elasticity coefficients is usually presented in absolute values. The **absolute value** of a number, denoted by two vertical bars on both sides of the number, is the value of the number without the positive or the negative sign.

Completely Inelastic. A completely inelastic demand means that the elasticity coefficient is zero. The elasticity coefficient is zero only if the value of the numerator in (6-1), which happens only if there is no change in the quantity demanded. Put differently, demand for a product is completely inelastic if the quantity of the product demanded remains unchanged, regardless of what happens to the price of the product. The demand curve that represents completely inelastic demand is vertical.

Examples of products for which the demand is almost completely, if not completely, inelastic include insulin, boxes of salt, boxes of matches, certain medical procedures such as a heart bypass operation, and cigarettes to true smokers. The quantities of these products demanded are expected to change little, if any, when the prices of these products change by a relatively small amount.

Please keep in mind that price change has to be small relative to the product price in order for the demand for the product to be completely inelastic. Since demand reflects ability as well as willingness to pay, every demand schedule becomes elastic if prices change by a significant amount. Consider insulin. If the price of insulin increases significantly, many diabetics will not be able to buy the medicine no matter how badly they may need it.

Relatively Inelastic. If the percentage change in quantity demanded is smaller than the percentage change in price for a product, the absolute value of the elasticity coefficient is less than 1, and the demand for the product is said to be relatively inelastic. When price changes, and when the resulting percentage change in quantity demanded is not as large as the percentage change in price, demand for the product is relatively inelastic. Products for which the demand is relatively or completely inelastic are sometimes called **necessities**.

Examples of products that are relatively price-inelastic include such products as city bus service, water, and bread in general rather than specific brands of bread. The demand curve that represents relatively inelastic demand is one comparatively, but not completely, vertical.

Relatively Elastic. A relatively elastic demand is the opposite case of the relatively inelastic demand in that the percentage change in quantity demanded is greater than the percentage change in price. When demand for a product is relatively elastic, a small percentage change in the price of the product leads to a larger percentage change in the quantity of the product demanded. Products for which the demand is relatively elastic are sometimes called **luxury** or **luxurious goods**. Examples of these products include fur coats, VCRs, and Johnnie Walker whisky.[1] The demand curve that represents relatively elastic demand is comparatively, but not completely, horizontal.

Completely Elastic. A completely elastic demand means that an infinitesimally small percentage change in price leads to an infinitely large percentage change in the quantity of the product demanded. The elasticity coefficient for completely elastic demand is infinity. *Ceteris paribus*, the more horizontal a demand curve is, the more elastic is the demand that the demand curve represents. A completely horizontal demand curve represents demand that is completely elastic.

Unit-Elastic. The elasticity coefficient for unit-elastic demand is -1. The elasticity coefficient will remain at one, only if a percentage change in price is offset by the corresponding percentage change in quantity demanded. If demand for a product is unit-elastic, percentage changes in the price of the product are offset by corresponding percentage changes in its quantity demanded, leaving the total revenue unchanged.

A percentage change in price is offset by the resulting percentage change in quantity, only if the area of a rectangle formed by a given combination of price and quantity is exactly the same as the area of another rectangle formed by another combination of price and quantity. Each of these rectangles represents total revenue from sales, since the area of a rectangle is obtained by multiplying price, and quantity demanded at a given price. The demand curve that represents unit-elastic demand is called the rectangular hyperbola, meaning a curve that results in rectangles of the same area under the curve.

Empirical Examples

As a person gets older, the person's needs for dental care also
increase. For children, on the other hand, dental care is still regarded by
many as a luxury good. Assuming that this description is accurate, one
would expect different price elasticities of demand for dental care
between adults and children. To be specific, demand for dental care is
expected to be inelastic for adults and elastic for children. This is exactly
what Willard Manning and Charles Phelps found in their study on the
demand for dental care.[2] According to Manning and Phelps, the price
elasticities of demand for dental visits are -0.65 for adult males, -0.78
for adult females, and -1.40 for children.

For another example, an article on import tariffs by Paarlberg and
Thompson provides sufficient information for us to derive an estimated
demand equation for U.S. wheat on the basis of 1975 to 1979 average
data:[3]

$$Q_w = 87.9041 - 0.0924P_w \qquad (6\text{-}8)$$

where the quantity is measured in millions of metric tons and the price
is the price per metric ton. For the same period of 1975 to 1979, the
average price per ton of wheat was $103.94. Plugging this price into
equation (6-8), we obtain the average quantity demanded for the period:

$$Q_w = 87.9041 - 0.0924(103.94)$$
$$= 78.30 \qquad (6\text{-}9)$$

Using the price elasticity formula (6-4),

$$E_p = (-0.0924) \times (103.94/78.30)$$
$$= -0.1227 \qquad (6\text{-}10)$$

This means that if the price of wheat were to increase by one percent
from $103.94 to $104.9794, the quantity of wheat demanded would have
decreased by 0.1227 percent from 78.30 to 78.204 million tons. As the

price of wheat changes, the price elasticity for demand will also change. Formula (6-4) makes it possible to compute price elasticities of demand for different price levels.

Determinants of the Price Elasticity

There are three main determinants of the price elasticity of demand: availability of substitutes, proportion of total expenditure for the product in the consumer's budget, and time.

Availability of Substitutes. Generally speaking, the larger the number of substitutes available for the product, the greater the price elasticity of demand for the product. Consider demand for new automobiles. Price elasticities of demand for new automobiles have been found by economists to be near -1.2, ranging from -1 to -2.[4] The empirical elasticity coefficients suggest that the demand for new automobiles in general is relatively, but not very, elastic.

Demand for individual models of new automobiles was found to be substantially more elastic. Professor Irvine, for instance, found that the price elasticity of demand for Ford Mustangs was -8.42.[5] If the price of a Ford Mustang falls by 1 percent with all other car prices remaining constant, the number of Mustangs demanded is expected to increase by 8.42 percent, rather than by the 1.2 percent found for new automobiles in general. Individual new car models have many more substitutes available in other new car models and used cars than do new automobiles in general.

The elasticity -8.42 does not mean that in reality Ford can increase sales of Mustangs by 8.42 percent by unilaterally lowering its price by 1 percent. If Ford lowers the price of the Mustang, manufacturers of other cars that are substitutes for Mustangs are also expected to lower their prices. The lower prices of substitutes for Mustangs will prevent sales of Mustangs from increasing significantly.

Portion of Budget. The larger the portion of income spent on a product in a consumer's budget, the greater the price elasticity of demand for the product. Consider a house priced at $100,000. If the price of the house increases by 10 percent, the difference between the old price and the new price is no less than $10,000, which will surely be noticed by most home buyers. Consider a pound of Morton salt priced at 20 cents. If the price per pound of salt increases by 10 percent, the difference between the old price and the new price is no more than 2 cents, which will hardly be noticed by any shopper. If the low-priced item is bought in a large quantity, however, the portion of money spent on the item is large in a consumer's budget, and the demand for the product becomes more elastic.

Another way of finding out how the proportion of one's budget spent on products determines the price elasticity of demand is to see how families with different levels of income treat a given product. According to the great economist Marshall, "The current prices of meat, milk and butter, wool, tobacco, imported fruits, and of ordinary medical attendance, are such that every variation in price makes a great change in the consumption of them by the working classes, and the lower half of the middle classes; but the rich would not much increase their own personal consumption of them however cheaply they were to be had. In other words, the direct demand for these commodities is very elastic on the part of the working and lower middle classes, though not on the part of the rich."[6]

Time. Demand for a product tends to be more elastic, the longer the time period under consideration. The effect of time on the price elasticity of demand works through the process in which consumers find and possibly develop tastes or preferences for other products that can be used as substitutes for the high-priced product. The longer the time period, the better the opportunities for consumers to find substitutes for the high-priced product. Long-run elasticities, therefore, tend to be more elastic than short-run elasticities.

Elasticities on a Given Demand Curve

Demand is inelastic at low prices or points below the midpoint of a straight-line demand curve, because, at low prices, consumers are not as sensitive to a given percentage change in price as they are to the same percentage change at high prices. Demand is elastic at high prices or points above the midpoint of the demand curve, because consumers are more sensitive to a given percentage change in price when prices are high. Demand is unit-elastic at the midpoint of the demand curve.

Price Elasticities and Total Revenue

Total revenue is the dollar value of all sales and is obtained by multiplying price by the quantity of sales. If 10 compact disc (CD) players were sold at a price of $200 each, total revenue would be $2,000. When the price of the CD player increases from $200 to $300, total revenue will increase if the number of CD players sold remains the same. Total revenue will also increase if the higher price is enough to make up for the decreased number of CD players sold. Whether total revenue increases or decreases with a price rise depends on the relative decrease in sales, which, in turn, depends on the price elasticity of demand. The relationships between price elasticities and total revenue are summarized in Table 6-1.

Table 6-1. Price Elasticity and Total Revenue

Elasticity	Price Changes	Total Revenue
Elastic	up	decrease
Elastic	down	increase
Unitary	up or down	no change
Inelastic	up	increase
Inelastic	down	decrease

Unit-elastic demand has an interesting property. Suppose that we start producing and selling a product. Suppose also that, in the absence of any comparable product, we have decided to charge a very low price in the beginning and raise the price gradually as the sales volume increases. At low prices, demand for our product is relatively inelastic. We raise price to increase total revenue. As the price reaches a level beyond the midpoint of the demand curve, demand for our product becomes elastic and total revenue starts declining. Total revenue is maximized when the demand for our product is unit-elastic.

Price Elasticity in Nonlinear Demand Functions

Linear demand functions are easy to follow, but not as practical as, say, a multiplicative demand function

$$Q = \alpha P^{\beta} \qquad (6\text{-}11)$$

The price elasticity of demand in (6-11) is obtained by applying (6-4) as follows:

$$
\begin{aligned}
E_P &= (dQ/dP) \times (P/Q) & (6\text{-}4)\\
&= (\beta\alpha P^{\beta-1}) \times (P/Q)\\
&= \beta\alpha P^{\beta}/Q\\
&= \beta. & (6\text{-}12)
\end{aligned}
$$

As we studied in Chapter 5, equation (6-11) is estimated using natural logarithms, *ln:*

$$ln\ Q = ln\ \alpha + \beta(ln\ P) \qquad (6\text{-}13)$$

The estimated value of β is the price elasticity of demand.

Generalizing the Elasticity Concept

The price elasticity of demand is the most important elasticity concept. There are other important elasticities, however. The other elasticities mentioned often in business and economics are the price elasticity of supply, the income elasticity of demand, and cross elasticities.

Price Elasticity of Supply

The price elasticity of supply measures suppliers' response in terms of percentage changes in the quantity supplied to percentage changes in the price of a product. The income elasticity of demand measures buyers' response in terms of changes in demand for a product when consumers' income changes. Since demand for normal products usually increases with rising income, the income elasticity for normal goods, like the price elasticity of supply, is expected to have a positive sign. The income elasticity for inferior goods, however, is negative.

Cross Elasticities

The cross (price) elasticity of demand is an elasticity that involves two different products. Suppose that there are two products, A and B. If the two products are related in some way, a change in the price of product A will affect the demand for product B. The **cross elasticity of demand** between two products measures percentage changes in demand for one product in response to percentage changes in the price of the other product.

Unlike other price elasticities, the sign of cross elasticity has a meaning. The sign tells us whether the two products are substitutes or complements. A **substitute** for a good or service is another good or service that satisfies the same wants, whereas a **complement** for a good or service is a good or service that is consumed together with the good or service under consideration. If the two products are unrelated, the elasticity coefficient is zero. A zero cross price elasticity means that changes in the price of one product have no effect on the demand for the other product.

Consider Terradex and Radtrak that are both detectors of radon, an odorless and colorless radioactive gas that causes lung cancer. Radon seeps into a house if a house is built on a lot that overlies uranium. The cross elasticity between Terradex and Radtrak is also positive because an increase in the price of Terradex results in an increase in demand for Radtrak.

Consider now golf clubs and a golf course, which are complements. The service of a golf course is priced by a greens fee. If the greens fee of a golf course is raised from $10 to $20 for 18 holes of play, the higher greens fee will have an adverse effect on the number of golf games played on the course and eventually on the number of new golfers. The higher greens fee will reduce the number of golf clubs purchased. The cross elasticity between fees for the service of a golf course and the number of golf clubs that golfers buy, therefore, is negative since the two move in the opposite direction. The sign of cross elasticity of demand for complements is negative.

A study by Rebecca L. Johnson and Daniel B. Suits on the demand for visits to U.S. national parks indicates that the gasoline price elasticity of demand for visits to national parks is -0.427. The same study found that the income elasticity of demand for visits to national parks was negative 0.885.[7]

Generalizing Estimation of Elasticities

Consider a demand function in which quantity demanded Q is assumed to depend upon price P and income Y. This demand function may be specified either as a linear equation (6-14) or as a nonlinear equation (6-15).

$$Q = a + b_1P + b_2Y + e \qquad (6\text{-}14)$$
$$Q = \alpha P^\beta Y^\gamma e \qquad (6\text{-}15)$$

Elasticity formula (6-4) allows us to estimate all elasticities suggested in equations (6-14) and (6-15). From linear demand function (6-14), we obtain the price and income elasticities:

$$E_P = b_1 \times (P/Q) \qquad (6\text{-}16)$$
$$E_Y = b_2 \times (Y/Q) \qquad (6\text{-}17)$$

From multiplicative demand function (6-10), we obtain the price and income elasticities:

$$E_P = \beta \qquad\qquad\qquad\qquad (6\text{-}12)$$
$$E_Y = \gamma \qquad\qquad\qquad\qquad (6\text{-}18)$$

Both specifications, (6-14) and (6-15), give us the elasticities. Which one we should use depends partly on which specification between the two gives us better estimates, and partly on whether we are interested in knowing elasticities at different price or income levels. If we feel that elasticities remain fairly stable over different price or income levels, it is customary to use the nonlinear specification in which the estimated coefficient is the elasticity.

Summary

The price elasticity of demand measures buyers' response, in terms of changes in the quantity demanded, to changes in the price of a good or service. The sign of the elasticity coefficient is determined even before the elasticity coefficient is computed. The sign is negative when the two variables, price and quantity demanded, change in the opposite direction. The sign is positive when the two variables involved change in the same direction. The elasticity coefficients is usually presented in absolute values.

The price elasticity of demand is classified into five categories. A completely inelastic demand has a zero elasticity coefficient and is represented by a vertical demand curve. If the elasticity coefficient is less than one, the demand for the product is relatively inelastic. A relatively inelastic demand curve is closer to a vertical line. A relatively elastic demand has an elasticity coefficient greater than one and is represented by a demand curve closer to the horizontal line. A completely elastic demand has an elasticity coefficient of infinity and is indicated by a horizontal demand curve. The unit-elastic demand has a unitary elasticity coefficient and is graphed as a rectangular hyperbola.

There are three main determinants of the price elasticity of demand: availability of substitutes, proportion of total expenditure for the product in the consumer's budget, and time. Generally speaking, the larger the number of substitutes available for the product, the greater the price elasticity of demand for the product. The larger the portion of income spent on a product in a consumer's budget, the greater the price elasticity of demand for the product. Demand for a product tends to be more elastic, the longer the time period under consideration.

The elasticity coefficients are different on different points of a straight-line demand curve. Demand is inelastic at points below the midpoint but elastic at points above the midpoint of the demand curve. Demand is unit-elastic at the midpoint of the demand curve. Total revenue increases if price is raised for an inelastic demand or if price is lowered for an elastic demand. Total revenue decreases if price is lowered for an inelastic demand or if price is raised for an elastic demand. Total revenue remains invariant to price changes if the demand is unit-elastic.

For an additive demand function, the price elasticity is estimated by multiplying the derivative of the quantity with respect to price by the ratio of price to quantity. For a multiplicative demand function, the estimated value of the power associated with the price variable is the price elasticity of demand.

Endnotes

1. Note that the word whisky spelled without the letter "e" refers to Scotch whisky, whereas whiskey spelled with an "e" refers to any whiskey, such as bourbon, which is not Scotch.
2. Willard G. Manning, Jr., and Charles E. Phelps, The demand for dental care, *Bell Journal of Economics*, 10 (Autumn 1979), pp. 503-525.
3. Philip L. Paarlberg and Robert L. Thompson, "Interrelated Products and the Effects of an Import Tariff," *Agricultural Economics Research*, 32 (October, 1980), pp. 21-32.
4. For empirical studies showing price elasticities of demand for new automobiles, see Daniel B. Suits, "The Demand for New Automobiles in the United States, 1929-1956," *Review of Economics and Statistics*, 53 (February 1971), 1-10; Senate

Subcommittee on Antitrust and Monopoly, "The Price Elasticity of Demand for Automobiles," in Edwin Mansfield (ed.), Microeconomics: Selected Readings, 2nd ed. New York: W. W. Norton, 1975, pp. 73-81; and F. Owen Irvine, Jr., "Demand Equations for Individual New Car Models Estimated Using Transaction Prices with Implications for Regulatory Issues," *Southern Economic Journal*, 49 (January 1983), 764-782.

5. Irvine, *ibid.*, p. 776.
6. Alfred Marshall, *Principles of Economics*, 8th ed. London: Macmillan, 1956, pp. 88-89.
7. Rebecca L. Johnson and Daniel B. Suits, "A Statistical Analysis of the Demand for Visits to U.S. National Parks: Travel Costs and Seasonality," *Journal of Travel Research*, 22 (Fall 1983), 21-24.

Chapter 7

Production

Production is an act of creating a good or service that has an exchange value. Building airplanes and submarines is a production activity; so is packaging pickles and steak sauce. Production is not limited to goods. Teaching, legal services, accounting services, and commercial entertainment such as stage shows and boxing matches are also production activities.

Production Function

Production processes typically require many different inputs. These inputs are broadly classified into land, labor, capital goods, and entrepreneurship. Each of these broad categories of inputs may be classified into more specific inputs. Labor, for instance, may be divided into hourly workers and salaried managers. A **production function** describes the relation between the quantity of output and various amounts of inputs needed to produce that quantity of output, given production technology. Assuming that the quantity of output (Q) depends on the amounts of labor (L) and capital (K), the production function is

$$Q = Q(L, K) \qquad (7\text{-}1)$$

In studies of production, inputs are classified into fixed inputs and variable inputs. **Fixed inputs** are those inputs whose quantity remains unchanged as the quantity of output changes. Fixed inputs include services of managers, physical plant capacity, and certain utilities such as safety lights and fixed monthly charges for telephone services. **Variable inputs** are those inputs that vary with the quantity of output. Variable inputs include most labor services and materials.

The presumption of the production function is that firms efficiently utilize all resources, including given technology, in order to obtain maximum output from given inputs. The relation between the quantity of output and inputs described in (7-1), therefore, is unique in that the quantity of output Q represents the maximum output that can be obtained from given inputs L and K. The process of combining different inputs in such a way as to obtain the maximum quantity of output from given inputs represents an optimization process that is central to all economic problems. The process of actually making a product is purely an engineering problem.

Product Concepts

Three product concepts are introduced in this section: total product, average product, and marginal product. For the sake of simplicity, let us assume that all inputs with the exception of labor are fixed in quantity, and that the labor input is measured in the number of workers. These assumptions considerably simplify our discussion by clarifying the amount of product that can be attributed to a particular input, labor.

Labor input is typically measured in hours. A **man-hour** is the labor service provided by a person for production for one hour. A **man-year** is the labor service provided by a person for production for a year. Another term used interchangeably with man-year is the **FTE**, which stands for the **full-time equivalent** and measures the amount of labor service that is equivalent to a man-year. If one person works full-time during the first half of the year and another person works full-time for the second half of the year, the total labor service by both persons is one FTE.

Defining Product Concepts

Total product of labor (Q) is the maximum quantity of output obtainable from a given number of workers with given capital goods that the workers work with. The **average product of labor** (Q/L) is the quantity of output per worker, obtained by dividing the total quantity of output by the number of workers. The **marginal product of labor** (dQ/dL) is the change in total product that is attributable to a unit change in labor services. The marginal product of labor usually means the quantity of output produced by the last worker hired. The term marginal in economics means one additional unit or one last unit added.

To economists, the term labor productivity may mean any of the three: total, average, or marginal products. To laypersons or news media, labor productivity usually means the average product of labor (Q/L). If the quantity of output per worker increases, labor productivity is said to be rising. If the quantity of output per worker decreases, labor productivity is said to be falling.

Short Run versus Long Run

The difference between the short run and the long run in laypersons' conversation is relative: the short run is a relatively short period of time, while the long run is a relatively long period of time. Economists sometimes use the two terms as they are used in laypersons' conversation. In studies of production and costs of production, however, economists make a clear distinction between the two terms that cannot necessarily be measured in lengths of a time period.

The **short run** in production refers to a period of time during which at least one input is fixed in amount and at least one input is variable so that the rate of output can be changed. The **long run** in production refers to a period of time during which all inputs vary. Stated in simple terms, the productive capacity remains unchanged in the short run but changes in the long run. Let us illustrate.

A candy store and a hamburger shop are located adjacent to each other on Main Street in Anytown. Suppose that sales at the hamburger shop have been increasing rapidly during the past six months, but sales at the candy store have been very slow during the same period. As more customers come to the hamburger shop, the shop hires more workers to make more hamburgers and cater to the increasing number of customers. Hiring more workers and selling more hamburgers with the given productive capacity are short-run changes.

Suppose that one day the owners of the hamburger shop decide to buy the adjacent candy store for expansion. From the moment that the decision to buy and sell the candy store has been signed by owners of the hamburger shop and owners of the candy store, the hamburger shop enters a long-run adjustment, which ends on the day when the expansion is completed and the expanded facility is open for business. Once the long-run change is over, the hamburger shop returns to the short-run operation.

The short run is an operating concept in that it involves day-to-day operations with a fixed capacity, while the long run is a planning concept in that the productive capacity is changed for increased production and possibly for lower unit costs of production. All inputs are variable in the long run since fixed inputs such as the size of a plant are no longer fixed during the long-run adjustment of a firm's expansion, or contraction, of its productive capacity.

Law of Diminishing Returns

An interesting question involving production in the short run is what happens to the quantity of output when more units of a variable input such as labor are added to the firm's fixed inputs? As use of fertilizer increases, crop yields increase, but not forever. If too much fertilizer is used, crops burn and crop yields actually decrease.

According to the **law of diminishing returns**, as successive units of a variable input are added to fixed inputs, the marginal product that is attributable to each additional unit of the variable input eventually declines. Returning to production function (7-1)

$$Q = Q(L, K) \qquad\qquad\qquad (7\text{-}1)$$

the law of diminishing returns can be stated as

$$dQ/dL > 0; \text{ and } d^2Q/dL^2 < 0 \qquad (7\text{-}2)$$
$$dQ/dK > 0; \text{ and } d^2Q/dK^2 < 0 \qquad (7\text{-}3)$$

In (7-2), the positive first derivative means that as the amount of labor input is increased while holding the amount of capital input constant, the quantity of output increases. The negative second derivative means that as the amount of labor input increases, the quantity of output increases at a decreasing rate. The decreasing rate led to the term "diminishing returns." Expressions in (7-3) indicate that as the amount of capital increases, the quantity of output increases at a decreasing rate.

Since the law of diminishing returns requires the presence of fixed inputs, the concept is a short-run concept. In contrast, the concept of returns to scale, introduced later in this chapter, is a long-run concept, since it assumes that the quantities of all inputs change.

Optimal Use of Inputs

Firms optimize the use of inputs in such a way to maximize the quantity of output for given inputs, or to minimize the use of inputs to produce a given quantity of output. The question is: How should a firm mix inputs in order to optimize their use?

Isoquant

To answer the question, consider a two-input case, labor (L) and capital (K). In Figure 7-1, the quantity of labor is shown on the vertical axis and the quantity of capital on the horizontal axis. we draw a curve that shows a schedule of all input combinations that can be used to produce a certain level of output. Since every point on the curve represents an equal quantity of output, the curve is called the *isos* (equal in Greek) and *quantitas* (quantity in Latin), i.e., **isoquant** curve.

The isoquant curve is convex to the origin because of the law of diminishing returns. In order to keep the level of output constant, the

amount of one input must be increased in use if the amount of the other
input is decreased in use because of diminishing returns of the input this
is increased in use.

   In Figure 7-1, the quantity of output at point A is produced with L_A
units of labor and K_A units of capital, while the same quantity of output
at point B is produced with L_B units of labor and K_B units of capital.

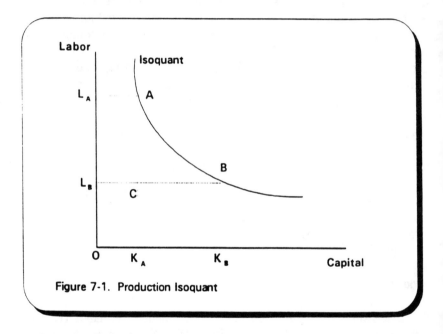

Figure 7-1. Production Isoquant

   Suppose that we want to move from point A to point B. Instead of
sliding down along the isoquant curve, we assume that we first move to
point C and then move to point B. When we move from point A to point
C, the amount of labor declines but the amount of capital remains the
same. The quantity of output at point C, therefore, is smaller than the
quantity of output at point A. How much smaller?

The decrease in the quantity of output when we move from A to C can be measured by the (decreased) change in the units of labor (dL) multiplied by the quantity of output that each of these units of labor no longer in use contributed before the move. The quantity of output per last units of labor is the marginal product of labor (MP_L). The decrease in the quantity of output is

$$dL \times MP_L \qquad\qquad (7\text{-}4)$$

The increase in the quantity of output obtained when we move from point C to point B is obtained similarly:

$$dK \times MP_K \qquad\qquad (7\text{-}5)$$

Ignoring the sign of change, the quantity decreased when we move from A to C must be equal to the quantity increased when we move from C to B, since points A and B remain on the same isoquant curve. That is

$$dL \times MP_L = dK \times MP_K \qquad\qquad (7\text{-}6)$$

Rearranging,

$$dL/dK = MP_K/MP_L \qquad\qquad (7\text{-}7)$$

The expression dL/dK is the slope of the isoquant. Expression (7-7) indicates that the slope of the isoquant curve is the ratio of marginal products of the two inputs, known as the **marginal rate of technical substitution** between the two inputs. Note in (7-7) that the slope of the isoquant depends on the ratio of the two marginal products, not on their absolute sizes.

Isocost

Production incurs costs. In Figure 7-2, a line, called the **isocost** schedule, is drawn to represent the total cost of purchasing labor and capital. The amount of labor that can be purchased when the total budget is spent to purchase labor input alone is the total budget (TB) divided by the price of labor (P_L) or wages. The maximum amount of labor that can be purchased with a given budget is indicated as TB/P_L on the vertical line. Similarly, the maximum amount of capital that can be purchased with a given budget is indicated as TB/P_K on the horizontal line.

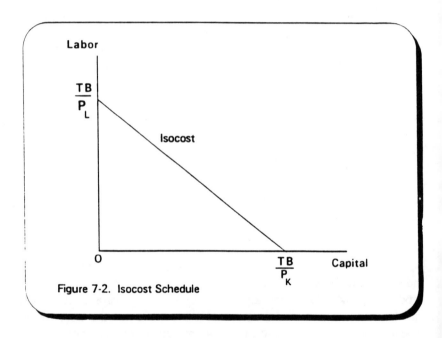

Figure 7-2. Isocost Schedule

In Figure 7-2, the slope of the isocost schedule is obtained by dividing the vertical intercept (TB/P_L) of the isocost schedule by its horizontal intercept (TB/P_K). That is,

$$\frac{TB}{P_L} \div \frac{TB}{P_K} = \frac{TB}{P_L} \times \frac{P_K}{TB} = \frac{P_K}{P_L} \qquad (7\text{-}8)$$

The slope of the isocost schedule is the ratio of two input prices.

Optimal Combination of Inputs

In a sense, isoquant curves represent alternative opportunities for production, while isocost schedules represent the ability to reach these alternative opportunities. To make the graphic solution easier to understand, consider two different cases. In one case, we have a fixed budget and try to maximize the quantity of output for this given budget. This case is graphed in Figure 7-3. In the other case, we have a given

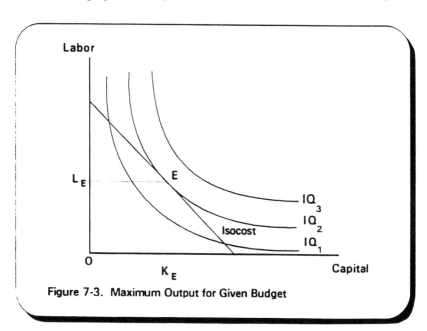

Figure 7-3. Maximum Output for Given Budget

quantity of output that we wish to produce at a minimum cost. This second case is graphed in Figure 7-4.

In Figure 7-3, we have one isocost schedule, indicating that the total budget is given at a level indicated by the isocost schedule. Production alternatives, however, are numerous depending on how we combine the two inputs, labor and capital. The point that represents the optimal use of inputs is indicated as E at which the isoquant curve (IC_2) is tangent to the isocost schedule. The quantity of output indicated by IC_3 is beyond the given budget, while other lower levels of output in IC_1 can also be produced with the given budget. However, the quantity of output indicated by the isoquant that is tangent to the isocost schedule is the maximum quantity of output that can be obtained with the given budget. Point E, therefore, indicates the optimal use of inputs at L_E and K_E.

At Point E, the slope of the isoquant curve dL/dP is equal to the slope of the isocost schedule, which is P_K/P_L. That is,

$$dL/dK = P_K/P_L \qquad (7\text{-}9)$$

Since in (7-7)

$$dL/dK = MP_K/MP_L$$

We obtain from (7-9) and (7-7)

$$MP_K/MP_L = P_K/P_L$$
$$MP_K/P_K = MP_L/P_L \qquad (7\text{-}10)$$

According to (7-10), in order to maximize the quantity of output for a given level of inputs, inputs should be combined in such a way that the marginal product of capital per dollar spent on capital be equal to the marginal product of labor per dollar spent on labor.

The process of minimizing the costs of producing a given quantity of output is demonstrated in Figure 7-4. In this case, we have one isoquant curve indicating the quantity of output that we plan to produce. There are, however, a several isocost schedules that can be used to produce the given quantity of output. As was the case in Figure 7-3, the optimal solution is again found at point E at which the given isoquant curve is tangent to the isocost schedule (IC_2) that represents the minimum cost. At point E, the slope of the isocost schedule is equal to the slope of the isoquant curve, leading us back to the optimal condition spelled out in (7-10). At point E, we use L_E units of labor and K_E units of capital and product the quantity of output indicated by the isoquant curve.

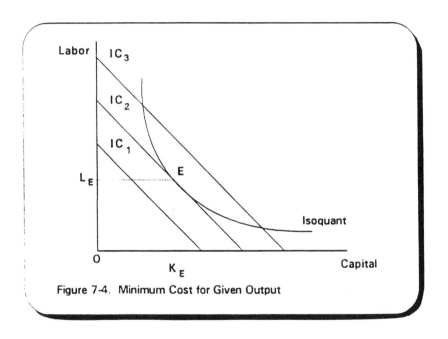

Figure 7-4. Minimum Cost for Given Output

Returns to Scale

An interesting question involving production in the long run is: What happens to the quantity of output when all inputs are varied simultaneously? Will the quantity of output increase at a faster or a slower rate than increases in inputs? When all inputs are varied simultaneously more or less in equal proportion, the **scale of production** is said to change. The primary concern in long-range planning is to find out what happens to the quantity of output as the scale of production changes. Changes in output that result from changes in the scale of production are called **returns to scale**.

Consider production function (7-1)

$$Q = Q(L, K) \qquad\qquad (7\text{-}1)$$

Suppose that we increase the amounts of labor and capital by a certain factor λ (called lambda):

$$Q(\lambda L, \lambda K) \qquad\qquad (7\text{-}11)$$

If we can factor out λ in (7-11), we obtain

$$\lambda^n Q(L, K) \qquad\qquad (7\text{-}12)$$
$$= \lambda^n Q, \qquad\qquad (7\text{-}13)$$

since $Q = Q(L, K)$.

If λ can be factored out as in (7-12), the production function (7-1) is said to be homogeneous of degree n. Being able to factor out λ in (7-11) means that in expanding the production capacity, all inputs have to be increased more or less in direct proportion.

In (7-13), whether the quantity of output (Q) increases faster or slower than the rate of increase of inputs (L and K) depends on the value of n, known as the degree of homogeneity or the scale coefficient (SCE). The **scale coefficient** is the ratio of changes in the quantity of output to changes in the quantities of all inputs. We conclude:

> $n > 1$: increasing returns to scale
> $n = 1$: constant returns to scale
> $n < 1$: decreasing returns to scale

Increasing returns to scale mean that the quantity of output increases faster than the increases in inputs; constant returns to scale mean that the quantity of output and the amounts of inputs increase at the same rate; and decreasing returns to scale mean that the quantity of output increases more slowly than the increases in inputs.

Suppose that the quantities of all inputs are doubled. If the quantity of output more than doubles, there are increasing returns to scale; if the quantity of output is also doubled, there are constant returns to scale; and if the quantity of output less than doubles, there are decreasing returns to scale.

The returns to scale for many industries have been estimated by several economists, including Douglas, Moroney, Waters.[1] These estimates indicate that production exhibits approximately constant returns to scale: A proportionate increase in the quantities of all inputs leads to a proportionate increase in the quantity of output.

Returns to Scale and
Cobb-Douglas Production Function

Consider a Cobb-Douglas production function specified often as a two-factor production function such as

$$Q = AL^aK^b \tag{7-14}$$

The Cobb-Douglas production function was developed by C. W. Cobb and Paul H. Douglas in the 1920s.[2] The better-known Douglas was an economist on the faculty of the University of Chicago and represented Illinois in the U.S. Senate from 1949 to 1967.

To determine the homogeneity and the degree of homogeneity of the Cobb-Douglas production function, we first multiply the inputs by λ

$$A(\lambda L)^a(\lambda K)^b \tag{7-15}$$
$$= A\lambda^aL^a\lambda^bK^b$$
$$= \lambda^{a+b}AL^aK^b$$
$$= \lambda^{a+b}Q, \text{ since } Q = AL^aK^b. \tag{7-16}$$

In order words, the Cobb-Douglas function is homogeneous of degree of the sum of a and b.

Summary

A production function describes the relation between the quantity of output and various amounts of inputs needed to produce that quantity of output, given production technology. The relation between the quantity of output and inputs in a production function is unique in that the quantity of output represents the maximum output that can be obtained from given inputs. Product concepts are divided into total product, average product, and marginal product. To economists, the term labor productivity may mean any of the three, but to laypersons or mass media, labor productivity usually means the average product of labor.

The short run in production refers to a period of time during which at least one input is fixed in amount and at least one input is variable so that the rate of output can be changed, while the long run refers to a period of time during which all inputs vary. According to the law of diminishing returns, as successive units of a variable input are added to fixed inputs, the marginal product that is attributable to each additional unit of the variable input eventually declines.

A curve that shows a schedule of all input combinations that can be used to produce a certain level of output is called an isoquant. The slope of the isoquant curve is known as the marginal rate of technical substitution between the two inputs. An isocost represents the total cost of purchasing different inputs needed to produce the output. An optimal combination of inputs is achieved when the isoquant curve is tangent to the isocost schedule. Put differently, in order to maximize the quantity of output for a given level of inputs, inputs should be combined in such a way that the marginal product of input A per dollar spent on input A be equal to the marginal product of input B per dollar spent on input B.

Returns to scale are divided into three. Increasing returns to scale in which the scale coefficient is greater than one mean that the quantity of output increases faster than the increases in inputs; constant returns to scale where the scale coefficient is one mean that the quantity of output and the amounts of inputs increase at the same rate; and decreasing returns to scale in which the scale coefficient is less than one mean that the quantity of output increases more slowly than the increases in inputs. If all inputs have to increase in direct proportion as the quantity of output is increased in the long run, the production function is said to be homogeneous. The Cobb-Douglas function is homogeneous of degree of the sum of the power coefficients.

Endnotes

1.   Paul H. Douglas, "Are there laws of production?" *American Economic Review*, 38 (March 1948) 1-41; John R. Moroney, "Cobb-Douglas production functions and returns to scale in U.S. manufacturing industry," *Western Economic Journal*, 6 (December 1967) 39-51; and A. A. Walters, "Production and cost functions: An econometric survey," *Econometrica*, 31 (January-April 1963) 1-66.
2.   Paul H. Douglas, *The Theory of Wages*, New York: Macmillan, 1924, pp. 132-135.

Chapter 8

Costs of Production

Costs represent the other side of production. The possibility that a given resource can be used to produce any one of a number of different products suggests that costs of production are an opportunity cost. **Opportunity cost** is the amount of other products that must be forgone to produce a given product. If a given quantity of a resource is used to build a new house, the construction of the house will necessarily require sacrifice of other products that could be produced with the same quantity of the same resource. The true economic cost of building the house, therefore, is not how much money is spent to build the house, but the value of alternative opportunities forgone due to the decision to build the house.

Cost Function and Concepts

A **cost function** describes the relation between costs of production (C) and levels of output (Q). That is,

$$C = f(Q) \qquad\qquad (8\text{-}1)$$

The presumption of the cost function is similar to that of the production function: that firms efficiently use resources to minimize the costs of producing a given output. The relation between costs and output described in equation (8-1) is unique in that the cost C represents the minimum cost needed to produce a given level of output.

Explicit versus Implicit Costs

Some production costs are explicit, while others are not. **Explicit costs** are the portion of the opportunity costs that is made in cash expenditures, while **implicit costs** are the portion of the opportunity costs that is not made in cash expenditures. Consider $1,000 that is held at a firm, rather than deposited at a bank. There are costs involved in holding the money at a firm; the costs are the amount of interest earnings that are sacrificed by holding the money at a firm.

Short-Run Cost Concepts and Curves

Cost concepts that individual firms utilize in day-to-day operations to optimize use of scarce resources are all short-run costs. Short-run costs are costs of production in which the quantity of at least one input, known as the fixed input, remains unchanged as the level of output changes. In practical terms, short-run costs refer to all types of costs that vary with the level of output while the capacity of production remains constant. Short-run cost concepts and curves are utilized for studies on the behavior of firms and industries presented in the following three chapters.

Fixed versus Variable Costs

In our discussion of production, inputs were divided into fixed inputs and variable inputs. **Fixed costs** are the payments made in purchasing fixed inputs, while **variable costs** are the payments made in purchasing variable inputs. Fixed costs do not vary with the level of output, while variable costs do.

Sunk Costs

Knowing whether a particular cost is a fixed cost or a variable cost is important because fixed costs are usually sunk in the short run and play a rather interesting role in determining the optimal course of action.

Sunk costs refer to expenditures that are already made and thus are common to alternative decisions.

To illustrate the use of sunk costs in making managerial decisions, suppose that a consulting firm spent $30,000 to prepare a project proposal. The total amount of the project requested is $100,000, but the granting agency is willing to offer only $80,000. We assume that cost estimates other than those already spent are $70,000. Even if the firm does not accept the offer, the $30,000 used to prepare the proposal has already been spent, or sunk, and cannot be recovered. In this case, the firm would be wise to accept any amount that is equal to or greater than $70,000. Any amount exceeding $70,000, will contribute to the payment already made to prepare the proposal.

Successful consulting firms spend a large sum of money to prepare the proposal, thus increasing the probability of obtaining the project and also the risk of a larger loss if the project is not obtained.

For another example, consider Golden Lamp Company that has 5,000 obsolete desk lamps that are carried in inventory at a manufacturing cost of $50,000. If the lamps were reworked for $20,000, they could be sold for $35,000. Alternatively, the lamps could be sold in their present conditions for $8,000 to a jobber located in a distant city. In a decision model analyzing these alternatives, the (sunk) cost that should not be considered is the manufacturing cost $50,000.

Total, Average, and Marginal Costs

The primary objective of studying cost concepts is to improve our ability to optimize the use of resources by minimizing costs of producing a given quantity of output. These relations among cost concepts are summarized:

$$TC = FC + VC \qquad (8\text{-}2)$$
$$AFC = FC/Q \qquad (8\text{-}3)$$
$$AVC = VC/Q \qquad (8\text{-}4)$$
$$AC = AFC + AVC \qquad (8\text{-}5)$$
$$\quad = TC/Q \qquad (8\text{-}6)$$
$$MC = dTC/dQ \qquad (8\text{-}7)$$

Cost Curves in the Short Run

The short-run cost curves used most often in studying the pricing behavior of individual firms are those of average cost, average variable cost, and marginal cost. The average cost, average variable cost, and marginal cost curves are graphed in Figure 8-1.

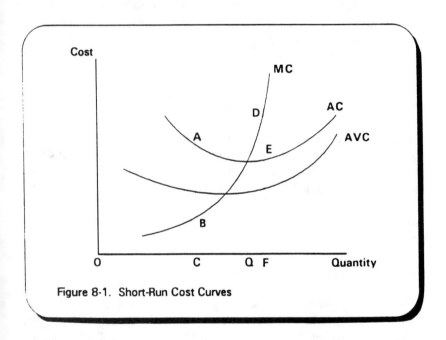

Figure 8-1. Short-Run Cost Curves

Reading the Graph

In Figure 8-1, we use the vertical axis to plot costs and the horizontal axis to plot the corresponding level of output. All three curves are said to have a U-shape for their decreasing and then increasing nature. Cost curves decrease until the amount of variable inputs is increased to the optimal level that fixed inputs require for their most efficient use. When the amount of variable inputs exceeds the optimal level, cost curves start rising because of the law of diminishing returns.

The vertical difference between the average cost curve and the average variable cost curve represents average fixed cost since average cost is the sum of average variable cost and average fixed cost. The average fixed cost decreases as the quantity of output increases, causing the vertical distance between the two curves to become narrower.

Relation between AC and MC Curves

Another interesting characteristic of the cost curves in Figure 8-1 is that the marginal cost curve crosses the lowest points of the average variable cost and the average cost curves. Let us concentrate on the average cost and the marginal cost curves to understand why the marginal cost curve crosses the lowest points of the cost curves.

The distance OQ in Figure 8-1 represents the quantity of output that corresponds to the lowest point of the average cost curve. For output levels, such as OC, that are less than OQ, the vertical distance BC, which measures marginal cost at the OC level of output, is smaller than the vertical distance AC, which measures average cost at the OC level of output. Assume the marginal cost for an additional unit of output is smaller than the average cost of all preceding units of output. Also assume the additional unit is added to all preceding units to compute the new average cost. Then the average cost newly computed after the additional unit is added to all preceding units would be smaller than the average cost for all preceding units alone.

For output levels, such as OF, that are greater than OQ, the vertical distance DF that represents marginal cost is greater than the vertical distance EF that represents average cost. Assume the marginal cost for an additional unit of output is greater than the average cost of all preceding units of output. Also assume the additional unit is added to all preceding units to compute the new average cost. Then the average cost newly computed after the additional unit is added to all preceding units would be greater than the average cost for all preceding units.

For another explanation, suppose that the average weight of all of us in this classroom is 150 pounds. Suppose that another person enters our classroom, and she is Twiggy, weighing 80 pounds. When the marginal weight of Ms. Twiggy is added and the average weight of the entire class is computed again, the new average weight will be smaller than 150 pounds. Consider the opposite case. Suppose that the new person who joins us is not Twiggy but a lineman of a professional football team, who weighs 300 pounds. After the football player's weight is added, the new average weight of the class will be greater than 150 pounds.

To summarize, if marginal cost is smaller than average cost, the average cost declines; if marginal cost is greater than average cost, the average cost increases. The marginal cost curve, therefore, crosses the lowest point of the average cost curve, and at the lowest point of the average cost curve, the average cost is equal to the marginal cost.

Using the quotient rule of differentiation, we can easily prove that the marginal cost and the average cost are equal at the lowest point of the average cost curve. Consider total cost function

$$TC = f(Q) \qquad\qquad (8\text{-}8)$$

The corresponding average cost function is

$$AC = TC/Q = f(Q)/Q \qquad\qquad (8\text{-}9)$$

Taking the first derivative of AC with respect to Q,

$$
\begin{aligned}
dAC/dQ &= [Qf'(Q) - f(Q)]/Q^2 \\
&= 1/Q[f'(Q) - f(Q)/Q] \\
&= 1/Q(MC - AC) \qquad\qquad (8\text{-}10)
\end{aligned}
$$

At the lowest point of the average cost curve, its slope has to be zero;

$$dAC/dQ = 1/Q(MC - AC) = 0 \qquad\qquad (8\text{-}11)$$

The slope is zero only if (MC - AC) = 0, since Q cannot be zero. This means that MC equals Ac at the lowest point of the AC curve.

Minimum Cost of Production

Recall the premise of the cost function: that firms efficiently utilize all resources in order to minimize costs in producing a given output. This means that every point on the average cost curve represents the minimum cost that is needed to produce the quantity of output indicated by the point.

Costs of Production in the Long Run

Short-run cost curves show minimum costs of production for given levels of output, provided that the capacity of production is fixed. Long-run cost curves, on the other hand, show minimum costs of production for given levels of output when the capacity of production is allowed to change. Put differently, long-run cost curves show minimum costs of production for different plant capacities.

Long-run cost curves make practical sense if the demand for a firm's product is large enough to make alternative plant capacities worth considering. The main objective of studying long-run cost curves is to determine the optimal capacity of production as indicated by the lowest per unit cost of production. In this section we study three issues that relate to the optimal capacity of production.

Economies and Diseconomies of Scale

By definition, the long-run average cost curve and the long-run average variable cost curve are identical, since fixed cost items such as plant size are allowed to vary, and thus there are no fixed costs in the long run.

Unlike the U-shape of short-run cost curves, which is explained by the law of diminishing returns, the U-shape of long-run cost curves is explained by economies of scale and diseconomies of scale. **Economies**

of scale refer to decreasing average costs of production made possible by a larger scale operation, while **diseconomies of scale** refer to increasing average costs of production due to problems arising from a scale that is too large for efficient management.

Factors that contribute to economies of scale include specialization of workers in job assignments, use of technologically efficient machines and equipment, possible use of by-products, and quantity discounts in purchase of inputs. All these advantages are made possible because of large-scale operation. If the scale of production is too large, however, diseconomies set in because of problems involving control and coordination of a firm's operations. The concept of economies of scale in costs corresponds to increasing returns to scale in production, whereas the concept of diseconomies of scale in costs corresponds to decreasing returns to scale in production.

Minimum Efficient Scale

As a firm expands its capacity of production, the per-unit cost of production is expected to decrease due to economies of scale. As a firm overexpands its capacity, however, the per-unit cost of production may increase due to diseconomies of scale. The production scale to which we turn our attention now is one at which per-unit cost of production is minimized, shown by the lowest point on the long run average cost curve.

The **minimum efficient scale** is the smallest level of output at which a firm's long-run average cost is minimized. For large manufacturing industries such as aluminum, automobile, coal, paper, and steel, the minimum efficient scale tends to be large. For other industries such as beauty salons, taverns, and electronics repair stores, the minimum efficient scale tends to be rather small.

The concept of the minimum efficient scale is important because eventually the minimum efficient scale determines the number of firms surviving in a given area for any particular industry. If the minimum efficient scale is large relative to total market demand for the product, only a few firms are likely to survive competition in the long run. If the minimum efficient scale is small relative to total market demand for a product, there will be many firms or stores that sell similar products.

Although many industries can easily be characterized by large or small minimum efficient scales, the minimum efficient scale of a given industry may change over time as technology improves. To see this trend of changing minimum efficient scales, let us consider the beer industry.

From 1950 to 1983, the number of independent U.S. brewing companies decreased from 369 to 33, while the sizes of surviving firms increased dramatically. The annual output of an average-sized firm increased from approximately 0.24 to 5.90 million barrels from 1950 to 1983. One barrel of beer contains 31 gallons of beer. According to Tremblay, these changes caused the five-firm concentration ratio to increase from 23.4 to 83.5 percent.[1]

The reason for the increased size of an average firm was technological improvements in production, including faster packaging equipment and greater plant automation that caused scale economies to rise. For example, modern canning lines fill 2,000 twelve-ounce cans per minute, whereas a typical high-speed canning line operated at a rate of just 300 cans per minute in 1952. In order to keep canning lines operating efficiently, it is estimated that a brewer would have had to increase plant production from 0.3 million barrels in 1952 to 2.2 million barrels in 1986. The minimum efficient scale of a modern brewing company is believed to be larger than 2.2 million barrels, since there are other advantages such as advertising efficiency that can be realized with a large-scale operation.

In the 1990s, a new technology allowed micro breweries to emerge. Micro breweries compete against giant brewery firms by differentiating the taste.

Economies of Scope

An important concept in production that is similar to economies of scale is the economies of scope. **Economies of scope** refer to situations in which the cost of producing two products in combination is smaller than the total cost of producing each product separately.[2] That is,

$$C(Q_1, Q_2) < C(Q_1, 0) + C(0, Q_2) \qquad (8\text{-}12)$$

where $C(Q_1, Q_2)$ = cost of producing both Q_1 and Q_2
$\qquad C(Q_1, 0)$ = cost of producing Q_1 only
$\qquad C(0, Q_2)$ = cost of producing Q_2 only.

Economies of scope usually arise in the production of several products that are complementary in production. For example, if the production of one good Q_1 generates a by-product that can be sold separately or used as an input in the production of another good Q_2, there will be economies of scope and a decrease in the average cost of producing both products.

Economies of scope are characteristic of a firm that produces several products. Economies of scope may also apply to the multi-plant firm, so long as separate plants can benefit from cost reductions by sharing such vital services as advertising, purchasing, market research, management of human resources, and transportation facilities.

The degree of economies of scope (S) is measured by

$$S = \frac{C(Q_1, 0) + C(0, Q_2) - C(Q_1, Q_2)}{C(Q_1, Q_2)} \qquad (8\text{-}13)$$

in which $S \leq 0$ indicates the absence of economies of scope, and $S > 0$ indicates the existence of economies of scope. "S" measures the percentage reduction in cost as a result of joint production.

Economic Order Quantity

Businesses carry inventories for many reasons. Manufacturers need to keep a stock of raw materials, unfinished goods in process, and finished goods to protect against uncertainties of delivery or work disruption. Retailers carry inventories to smooth out fluctuations in consumer demand.

Businesses incur costs in carrying inventories. These costs are of two broad types; carrying cost and ordering cost. The behavior of these two costs vary depending on how businesses order the additional quantity for inventory.

Basically, the business has two choices in ordering. The business may order a larger quantity and place fewer orders during a year. In this case, the carrying cost will be higher but the ordering cost will be lower. Alternatively, the business may order a smaller quantity and place orders more frequently during a year. In this case, the carrying cost will be lower but the ordering cost will be higher. It is obvious that there has to be an optimal combination of the quantity ordered and the number of orders placed during a year that can minimize the total cost of managing the inventory. We are back to an optimization problem.

To develop a model of inventory management, let us make assumptions: that the retailer knows in advance the amount of sales during a year; that the demand for the product is uniform during the year; and that the price of the product is predetermined. The total inventory cost (TIC) is the sum of carrying cost and ordering cost. Carrying costs include utilities for the storage room, taxes on inventory, labor costs for guarding and maintaining the inventory, and interest payments on loans incurred to build the storage room. Ordering costs, on the other hand, include fax and long distance call expenses, bookkeeping and shipping costs.

The carrying cost is the carrying cost per unit (k) multiplied by the half of the quantity ordered (Q/2) each time the order is placed. The half of the quantity ordered represents the average inventory that the firm is maintaining during a given period. It is the half since on day one, the inventory is the total quantity ordered, while on the last day the inventory is zero. During day one and the last day, the inventory is depleted uniformly according to the assumptions we made.

The ordering cost has two components; fixed cost of ordering and variable cost of ordering. The fixed cost of ordering is the fixed cost of ordering per order (f) multiplied by the number of orders during a year (S/Q) that is obtained by dividing the total annual sales (S) by the quantity ordered (Q) each time an order is placed. The variable cost of ordering is the variable cost per unit (v), such as a shipping cost per unit, multiplied by the total quantity of sales during a year (S). To summarize,

$$TIC = k(Q/2) + f(S/Q) + vS \qquad (8\text{-}14)$$

where TIC = total inventory cost
   k = carrying cost per unit
   Q = quantity ordered
   f = fixed cost of ordering per order
   S = total annual sales
   v = variable cost of ordering per unit of the product.

The problem is to find the quantity, called the **economic order quantity,** that minimizes the total inventory cost. This is a straightforward optimization problem. The first-order condition is obtained by taking a partial derivative of TIC with respect to changes in Q, while the second-order condition is tested by taking the second derivative of TIC with respect to changes in Q.

In order to take the derivatives of TIC, we rearrange equation (8-14):

$$TIC = (k/2)Q + fSQ^{-1} + vS \qquad (8\text{-}15)$$

Taking the derivatives of (8-9) and solving for Q,

$$
\begin{aligned}
\partial TIC/\partial Q &= k/2 - fSQ^{-2} + 0 \qquad (8\text{-}16)\\
&= k/2 - fS/Q^2 = 0\\
k/2 &= fS/Q^2\\
kQ^2 &= 2fS\\
Q^2 &= 2fS/k\\
Q &= \sqrt{(2fS/k)} \qquad (8\text{-}17)
\end{aligned}
$$

Solution (8-17) indicates that the total inventory cost is minimized when the quantity ordered each time an order is placed is equal to the square root of twice the product of fixed cost of ordering (f) and annual sales (S), divided by the carrying cost per unit.

To test the second order condition, we take the second derivative of TIC with respect to changes in Q in (8-15). This is the same as taking an another first derivative in (8-16):

$$\partial^2 TIC/\partial Q^2 = 0 + 2fSQ^{-3}$$
$$= +2fS/Q^3 \qquad (8\text{-}18)$$

In (8-18), all variables are positive. Since $\partial^2 TIC/\partial Q^2 > 0$, the EOQ derived in (8-17) represents a minimum cost EOQ.

For illustration, suppose that the local Ford dealer expects to sell 1,000 Mustangs of the restyled 1994 model during the year. These sales (S) will be evenly spaced throughout the year. The cost of storing an unsold Mustang for one year is $150. The cost of placing a new order for Mustangs from Detroit is $100 plus $25 shipping per new Mustang ordered. The economic order quantity (Q) is obtained

$$Q = \sqrt{[2(100)(1000)]}/150$$
$$= 36.51 \text{ or } 37 \text{ Mustangs} \qquad (8\text{-}19)$$

The shipping cost does not enter the EOQ solution since it drops out in the first derivative. The optimal number of orders during the year is

$$S/Q = 1,000/37$$
$$= 27 \text{ orders.} \qquad (8\text{-}20)$$

If inventories run out, there is a **stockout**. To avoid a stockout, businesses may add a **safety stock** for surplus inventories.

Summary

A cost function describes the relation between costs of production and levels of output. The relation between costs and output in a cost function is unique in that the cost represents the minimum cost needed to produce a given level of output. Fixed costs are the payments made in purchasing fixed inputs, while variable costs are the payments made in purchasing variable inputs. Sunk costs refer to expenditures that are already made and thus are common to alternative decisions. Sunk costs do not enter the decision making process in the short run.

The cost curves are U-shaped because of the law of diminishing returns in the short run, and economies or diseconomies of scale in the long run. Economies of scale refer to decreasing average costs of production made possible by a larger scale operation, while diseconomies of scale refer to increasing average costs of production due to problems arising from a scale that is too large for efficient management. Firms are assumed to efficiently utilize all resources in order to minimize costs in producing a given output. Every point on the average cost curve, therefore, represents the minimum cost that is needed to produce the quantity of output indicated by the point. The minimum efficient scale is the smallest level of output at which a firm's long-run average cost is minimized. The minimum efficient scale determines the number of firms surviving in a given area for any particular industry.

The economic order quantity is the quantity of an order that minimizes the total inventory cost. In a simple model, the economic order quantity is equal to the square root of twice the product of fixed cost of ordering and annual sales, divided by the carrying cost per unit.

Endnotes

1.   Victor J. Tremblay, "Scale economies, technological change, and firm-cost asymmetries in the U.S. brewing industry," Quarterly Review of Economics and Business, 27 (Summer 1987) 71-86.

2.   For more on economies of scope, see John C. Panzar and Robert D. Willig, "Economies of Scale and Economies of Scope in Multi-Product Output Production," Bell Laboratories Economic Decision Paper No. 13, 1975; and William J. Baumol, "Scale Economies, Average Cost, and Profitability of Marginal Cost Pricing," in R. E. Grieson, ed., Essays in Urban Economics and Public Finance in Honor of William S. Vickery, D. C. Heath, 1975, pp. 43-57.

Chapter 9

Price and Output Decisions of Firms under Perfect Competition

Perfect competition is almost like Garrison Keillor's Lake Wobegon, the misty, imaginary Minnesota town that was the home for a show called A Prairie Home Companion, broadcast on public radio each Saturday for 13 years until 1987. What life was like in Lake Wobegon varied with the kind of dream that one wished to experience there. Just as Lake Wobegon provided some with an opportunity to dream of the kind of life that they wished they could have lived, so also does perfect competition provide some economists with an opportunity to dream of the kind of market that they wish that they could arrange. Elusive as that may be, it is still necessary to study perfect competition because it provides the basis for studying and, hopefully, for improving other more realistic markets.

All firms have to determine the price that they will charge for their product and the quantity of the product that they have to produce in order to maximize profits. Firms that operate in perfectly competitive markets are expected to make these decisions in a manner that is different from the manner in which firms operating under more realistic market conditions do. If we were to make markets increasingly more competitive, the way in which real firms determine their price and quantity of output would be more like the one in which firms in the conceptually perfectly competitive market make their decisions on price and output. By studying price and output decisions of firms operating under perfect competition, we hope to present the basis for making a judgment as to whether or not it is desirable, or even possible, to move toward more competitive markets. Incidentally, words ending in the suffix "-ics" (acoustics, politics, tactics, gymnastics, etc.) are regarded as either singular or plural, depending on meaning. When the word is being treated as a subject or science, it is construed as singular ("Tactics is among the subjects taught at West Point"). When the word denotes practical activities or qualities, it is construed as plural ("The tactics of the Battle of Gettysburg are studied at West Point").... By the way, economics is almost always construed as singular, perhaps because it is difficult to think of it in the sense of practical activities.[1]

Defining Perfect Competition

Perfect competition is defined as market conditions in which the demand for the output of every firm in a given industry is so perfectly elastic that each firm is a price taker for all quantities of output it produces. The usual requirements of perfect competition are: (1) a large number of sellers and buyers each of whom handles quantities so small relative to the market as a whole that no one seller or buyer can control the market price; (2) no barriers to entry into the market or exit from the market; (3) homogeneity of products sold by different sellers in the market, meaning that consumers perceive all of these products to be basically identical; (4) perfect knowledge of the market by all buyers and sellers such that everyone knows who is selling which product where at what price; and (5) perfect mobility of resources.

Firms must make decisions on what price to charge and how much to produce. Since firms operating under perfect competition are price takers, these firms charge the price that is determined in the market. The focus of decision-making in firms operating under perfect competition, therefore, is on determination of the level of output at which the firm maximizes profits.

Revenue Curves under Perfect Competition

Recall that demand curves show the relation between different prices and quantities demanded at these prices. The horizontal line also shows the relation between prices and quantities demanded at these prices, in the special case where there is only one price. The demand curve is always the same as the average revenue curve because both show the relation between prices and quantities sold at these prices. At this point, we may recall the price elasticity of demand. The demand curve for a product that is completely elastic was a horizontal line. The demand curve faced by a firm under perfect competition is completely elastic, and represents the firm's average revenue curve as well as its marginal revenue curve.

MR = MC for Profit Maximization

Firms produce goods and services to make profits. When markets are competitive, making profits may not be sufficient to ensure the survival of these firms. A favorite behavioral assumption that economists make when studying production activities of firms is that firms maximize, not simply make, profits. Profit is the difference between total revenue and total cost. Total cost refers to total economic costs, which include implicit as well as explicit costs.

Like costs, revenues from sales of goods and services are of three types: total revenue, average revenue, and marginal revenue. **Total revenue** (TR) is simply the dollar value of sales, obtained by multiplying price (P) by the quantity of sales (Q). **Average revenue** (AR) is total revenue divided by the quantity of sales. Average revenue is always the price of a product as long as all units of the product are sold at the same price. **Marginal revenue** (MR) is obtained when changes in total revenue are divided by the corresponding changes in the quantity of sales. To summarize,

$$TR = P \times Q \qquad\qquad (9\text{-}1)$$
$$AR = TR/Q \qquad\qquad (9\text{-}2)$$
$$MR = dTR/dQ \qquad\qquad (9\text{-}3)$$

Profits are maximized by producing a level of output at which the difference between total revenue and total cost is the greatest. The profit-maximizing level of output can also be determined, more conveniently, by equating marginal revenue and marginal cost.

Optimization of Profit

The profit-maximizing level of output can be determined by equating revenue and cost at the margin. To see why this is the case, profit (π) is stated as the difference between total revenue (TR) and total cost (TC):

$$\pi = TR(Q) - TC(Q) \qquad\qquad (9\text{-}4)$$

Taking the first derivative for the first-order condition

$$\begin{aligned} d\pi/dQ &= TR'(Q) - TC'(Q) \\ &= MR - MC = 0 \qquad\qquad (9\text{-}5) \end{aligned}$$

From (9-5), MR = MC at the optimal level of profit. Taking the second derivative of (9-4) for the second-order condition,

$$\begin{aligned} d^2\pi/dQ^2 &= TR'(Q) - TC'(Q) \\ &= MR' - MC' < 0 \end{aligned}$$

Or

$$MR' < MC' \qquad\qquad (9\text{-}6)$$

The optimal profit obtained in (9-5) is the maximum profit so long as the slope of marginal revenue is smaller than the slope of marginal cost.

How the MR = MC Rule Works

Marginal revenue is the revenue from production and sale of the last unit of output, while marginal cost is the cost of producing the last unit of output. The **MR = MC rule** states that profits are maximized when firms produce the level of output at which marginal revenue is equal to marginal cost. To understand how the equality between marginal revenue and marginal cost ensures maximization of profits for firms, let us superimpose in Figure 9-1 a typical marginal cost curve onto a horizontal marginal revenue curve. The horizontal marginal revenue curve means that the firms under our consideration operate under market conditions that are perfectly competitive. The following explanation holds equally true even if the demand curve is downward sloped rather than horizontal.

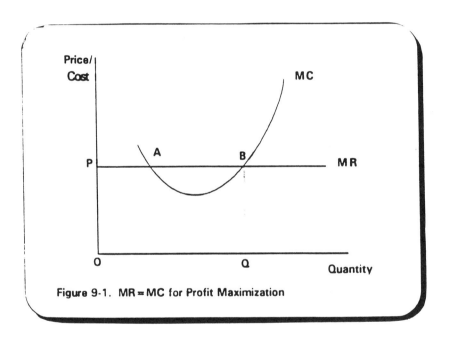

Figure 9-1. MR = MC for Profit Maximization

In Figure 9-1, MR is equal to MC at two points, A and B. At point A, the slope of the MC curve is negative and thus is smaller than the slope of the MR schedule which is zero. The quantity of output produced at point A does not maximize profit. If fact, profit is negative at point A. Only at point B, profit is maximized since the slope of MC is positive and thus is greater than the slope of the MR schedule which is zero.

A note of caution is in order. The MR = MC rule does not necessarily mean that the firm is making profits. What the rule says is that if the firm is making profits, the rule makes sure that the firm is maximizing profits; if the firm is losing money but continues to produce, the rule makes sure that the firm is minimizing losses. Whether the firm is making a profit or incurring a loss depends on the price of the product in relation to the average cost of production at the point where marginal revenue equals marginal cost. If the product price is greater than the average cost of production, the firm is maximizing profits. If the product price is smaller than the average cost of production, the firm is minimizing losses. The MR = MC rule is essentially a short-run rule, since no firm can survive long by only minimizing losses.

Combining the Cost and Revenue Curves

Profits are obtained by subtracting costs from revenues. To graphically show the process of determining the profit-maximizing level of output, it is necessary to superimpose cost curves and revenue curves. Cost curves and revenue curves of firms that operate under perfectly competitive markets are superimposed onto each other in Figure 9-2.

Price and Output Decisions Graphed

The height of the average revenue curve is the market price that is determined by demand and supply in the market. The price of the product, therefore, is OA. To find the quantity of output at which the firm maximizes profits, the MR = MC rule is applied. The point where marginal revenue equals marginal cost is D. To determine the quantity of output for profit maximization, we need to go to the horizontal axis that measures the quantity of output. We do this by drawing a line vertically from point D toward the quantity line. The point of intersection on the quantity line is G. The profit-maximizing quantity of output, therefore, is OG.

All readings of Figure 9-2 are summarized below. These readings are unique in that they relate to the profit-maximizing level of output:

price:	OA
average revenue:	GD or OA
marginal revenue:	GD or OA
quantity:	OG
total revenue:	OADG
average cost:	GE or OB
total cost:	OBEG
profit per unit:	ED or BA
profit:	BADE
average variable cost:	GF or OC
total variable cost:	OCFG
average fixed cost:	FE or CB
total fixed cost:	CBEF

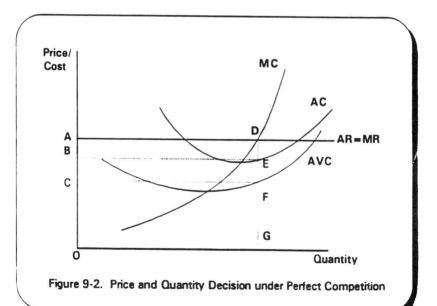

Figure 9-2. Price and Quantity Decision under Perfect Competition

Moving toward the Break-even Point

When firms in one industry make economic profits, firms in other industries begin to transfer resources to the market in which firms are enjoying economic profits. As more firms join the industry, the market supply curve shifts to the right and the market price falls. **Economic profits** are profits in excess of a normal rate of return. To understand how firms respond to changes in economic profits, we need to know what a normal rate of return is.

Normal Rate of Return

A **normal rate of return** is the rate of return that the firm would expect to make if the same amount of resources were invested in production of other goods or services. A most practical definition of the normal rate of return is the average rate of return on investment in all industries. To illustrate, suppose that firms manufacturing the gas pumps used at gas stations make 18 cents for every dollar invested before taxes are paid. The rate of return for these firms, then, is 18 percent. The rate of return on investment in U.S. manufacturing industries usually averages 10 to 15 percent on a pre-tax basis. Suppose that the average rate of return on investment in U.S. manufacturing industries is 12.5 percent. Firms manufacturing gas pumps are making economic profits of 5.5 percent, which is the difference between 18 percent for these firms and 12.5 percent for the average rate of return on investment in all industries.

If firms manufacturing gas pumps continue to make economic profits, more firms will join the industry, causing the supply of gas pumps to increase and their prices to fall. Likewise, if the production of computer software is profitable, more firms will produce software. If selling fur coats is profitable, more businesses will sell fur coats. If the rate of return on investment in the sale of fur coats falls below the average rate of return on investment in other industries, businesses selling fur coats will leave the industry.

If the market is highly competitive, the market price is expected to fall until it finally reaches the level that equals the lowest point of the average cost curve. At the lowest point, all firms make no more than normal profits, that is, the same level of profit as firms in all other industries make on an investment. The firm in Figure 9-3 responds to the falling market price from OA to OA' by reducing the quantity of output produced from OG to OG'.

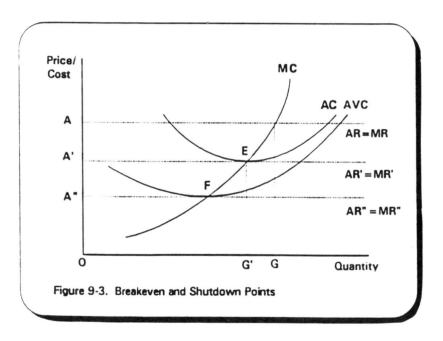

Figure 9-3. Breakeven and Shutdown Points

Production at the Break-even Point

When price equals the lowest average cost at point E in Figure 9-3, total revenue is equal to total cost. Point E is called the break-even point. Since the cost curves already include a normal rate of return, firms earn normal profits at the break-even point and have no incentive to leave the industry.

Shutdown Point and Loss Minimization

Firms do not always earn profits. Even profitable firms sometimes have to survive hard times. When new firms enter an industry in which existing firms earn economic profits, there is no assurance that the influx of new firms will stop as soon as the price falls to the break-even level. In a market system in which decisions on production are made by individual firms rather than one central agency, it is likely that the market will overreact to economic profits and the influx of new firms will continue until price falls below the break-even level. When price falls below the break-even level, firms incur losses. Firms do not usually shut down simply because they incur losses. When firms do not make profits but are still in business, firms optimize use of their resources by trying to minimize their losses.

Optimal Use of Resources under Losses

Suppose that a firm incurring a loss shuts down operations temporarily. Even if the firm does not produce, there will be a loss since expenditures on all fixed inputs will still have to be made. Rent or mortgage payments on property, interest on loans, property taxes, salaries of managers, and some utilities will all have to be paid, unless and until the firm completely goes out of business. In other words, if the firm shuts down temporarily, the amount of loss is equal to fixed cost.

Assuming that the loss is judged to be temporary, the firm will continue to produce so long as the amount of loss is equal to or less than the firm's fixed cost. If the loss exceeds the firm's fixed cost, the firm has two choices. One choice is to shut down. The other is to continue to operate in order to avoid the costs of returning to production since return would incur significant start-up costs in hiring new employees and attracting new customers.

Production at the Shutdown Point

Point F in Figure 9-3 is called the **shutdown point** because at a price below OA" the firm minimizes losses by shutting down its operation. At a price equal to OA", the amount of loss is equal to the fixed cost regardless of whether the firm continues operation or shuts down.

Shutdown point does not mean that competitive firms always shut down operations whenever price falls below the lowest point of the average variable cost. A shutdown occurs in this case, because we are assuming that the firm will choose to shut down if the loss is greater than the firm's fixed cost. In reality, firms may continue to produce if these firms judge that the long-term loss from the temporary shutdown exceeds the short-term gain.

Supply Curve of the Firm

Figure 9-3 shows clearly that the segment of the marginal cost curve on or above the lowest average variable cost curve represents the relation between prices and quantities supplied at these prices. The relation between prices and quantities supplied at these prices is the definition of the firm's supply curve. The segment of the marginal cost curve on or above the average variable cost curve, therefore, is the short-run supply curve of firms that operate under perfect competition.

Issues of Competitive Pricing

Some interesting issues arise from the process through which competitive firms make decisions on price and the quantity of output for profit maximization. Two such issues are marginal cost pricing and externalities.

Marginal Cost Pricing

For firms operating under perfect competition, price is equal to average revenue, which in turn is equal to marginal revenue. The average revenue and marginal revenue schedules of firms operating under perfect competition are identical. Firms determine the profit-maximizing level of output by equalizing marginal revenue and marginal cost. In other words, profit-maximizing firms operating under a completely elastic demand curve select price (P) at a level that is equal to marginal revenue, which in turn is equal to marginal cost (MC); that is, P = MC. The process of pricing a product according to P = MC is known as **marginal cost pricing**.

Marginal cost pricing is said to be economically efficient. To understand what this statement means, consider a careful shopper who finally selects a cassette tape of Symphony No. 5 by Ludwig van Beethoven and pays $15 for it. The price of the cassette tape is the maximum price that the consumer is willing to pay for the product in order to satisfy her wants. The product price thus measures the maximum benefit or satisfaction that the consumer derives from purchasing the tape.

The marginal cost of making the cassette tape, on the other hand, measures the minimum cost for Polydor International of producing the last unit of Beethoven Symphony No. 5 albums on cassette tape. The minimum cost represents the minimum amount of resource that the society is willing to give up in order to produce the product. If price is equal to marginal cost for a given product, the maximum price that consumers are willing to pay for the product is exactly equal to what the society has to forgo to produce the product.

If the price of a product is greater than the marginal cost of producing the product, consumers value the product more than the society is willing to sacrifice to produce the product, causing production of the product to increase. If the price of a product is less than the marginal cost of producing the product, the resources used to produce the product should be transferred to production of another higher priced product that consumers value more. When resources are transferred to production of another product that society values more, economic efficiency is improved. That is because the product valued more by the society is now produced instead of the product that the society values less.

To summarize, marginal cost pricing requires that demand price be made equal to marginal cost. Since resources are drawn away from alternative uses, marginal costs should accurately reflect the social opportunities forgone to produce a given product. The equality of price and marginal cost ensures that consumers equate marginal benefits from the use of given resources with the real alternatives forgone elsewhere. In a world of pure competition, the market mechanism would operate to ensure this equality.

The contention by economists that resources are most efficiently allocated when price is equal to marginal cost is based on certain conditions. The most important of these conditions is that there are no important spillover effects in production and consumption of the product that are not reflected in the marginal cost of producing the product. If there were spillover benefits, marginal cost would overestimate the true cost of producing the product; if there were spillover costs, marginal cost would underestimate the true cost of producing the product. Spillover effects, called also externalities, are explained in the next section.

Externalities

One of the major advantages of having markets that are perfectly competitive is that under perfect competition, price accurately measures other goods and services that society must sacrifice to produce the product under our consideration. When there are spillover effects, price no longer measures marginal cost accurately.

Consider chloroflorocarbons (CFC). CFC is widely believed to destroy the earth's ozone layer. Once released, CFC remains in the atmosphere for about 100 years destroying the atmosphere's ozone layer. The disappearance of the ozone layer is expected to increase the earth's temperature, cause more fires, cause skin cancer, and break the food chain, thereby reducing food production. Scientists believe that CFC is released through the burning of fossil fuels or the use of spray cans utilizing CFC's as a propellant.

An interesting economic problem stemming from these theories about CFC affects not only the firms that use fossil fuels and consumers who buy their products but also persons who are not a party to the trade. When firms using fossil fuels do not remove CFC before it is released into the atmosphere, the market prices of products produced by these firms underestimate the true cost of their production.

Effects of a trade between sellers and buyers on a third party who is not part of the trade are called **spillover effects** or **externalities**. In the case of flu shots or pesticides, the spillover effects are beneficial to society and thus are called **spillover benefits** or **external benefits**. In the case of water or air pollution and CFC, the spillover effects are detrimental to society and thus are called **spillover costs** or **external costs**. We can see how spillover effects such as pollution affect the allocation of resources by supposing that a power company pollutes water in the process of generating electricity. If the power company were to clean the water and add the cost of cleaning the water to the price per kilowatt hour of electricity, the price of electricity would be higher than it is now. In other words, when the power company is allowed to pollute water, the price of electricity is lower than it should be, and consumers are expected to use more electricity than they would be using if the price were higher. Allowing the power company to pollute water is equivalent to society allocating more resources to the generation of electricity than would have been allocated in the absence of externalities.

When firms pollute the environment, this does not necessarily mean that owners or managers of these firms are bad people. In a market that is highly competitive, the extra expenditure by one firm on cleaning up the pollution may influence the survival of the firm unless the expenditure is matched by other firms in the industry that also pollute the environment. The existence of externalities invites government to interfere with operations of the private sector. Government may force all firms to internalize external costs in a number of ways, including regulation by the Environmental Protection Agency and sale to firms of a permit to pollute the environment. Revenues from the sale of permits to pollute can then be used to clean up the environment.

Auctions and Bidding

A special case of a competitive market relates to auctions and bidding.[2] In the commonly used **English auction**, the price of an item is successively raised until only one bidder remains. The successful bidder pays slightly more than what the second most eager buyer is willing to pay. In a **Dutch auction**, the auction price starts very high and is reduced gradually until a person accepts the bid price. In a Dutch auction, the successful bidder pays the maximum that he or she is willing to pay without knowing how much any other buyer is willing to pay. The word auction is derived from the Latin *augere*, which means "to increase".

The English auction and the Dutch auction are "outcry" auctions. There are two additional types, which are "sealed" rather than "outcry" type. In the **first sealed bid auction**, the bidder who submits the lowest or the highest sealed bid wins at the bid price. The first sealed bid auction is similar to the Dutch auction in that both will have to reveal their **true reservation price**. In the **second sealed bid auction**, the bidder who submits the lowest or the highest sealed bid wins but at the second lowest or highest bid price. The second sealed bid auction is similar to the English auction in that the bidder does not have to reveal the true reservation price to win the bidding.

One of the most important biddings in terms of the bid amount relates to the auctioning of Treasury securities. **Treasury bills** have maturities of three months to one year. We buy them at a discount and get paid their full face value when they mature. **Treasury notes** mature in two to ten years. We are paid interest every six months until maturity. **Treasury bonds** have maturities of more than ten years up to 30 years. Treasury currently issues only 30-year bonds. Like Treasury notes, we are paid interest every six months until maturity.

For securities already issued, we can buy them from a brokerage or bank for a $30 to $50 fee. For new issues, we can buy them from a brokerage or bank, or directly from the nearest Federal Reserve Bank through the Treasury Direct system.

In auctions and bidding, bidders have to be careful to avoid the **winner's curse** in which the winning bidder wins the bid with the lowest cost estimate that turns out to be below the cost and the bidder loses money. The bidding price should not be below the true reservation price that represents the lowest cost estimate but still generates some profit.

Summary

Market is perfectly competitive when the demand for the output of every firm in a given industry is so perfectly elastic that each firm is a price taker for all quantities of output it produces. Requirements of perfect competition include a large number of sellers and buyers, no barriers to entry, homogeneity of products, perfect knowledge of the market, and perfect mobility of resources. The demand curve faced by a firm under perfect competition is completely elastic, and represents the firm's average revenue curve as well as its marginal revenue curve.

Firms optimize the use of resources by trying to maximize profits. Profits are maximized by producing a level of output at which the difference between total revenue and total cost is the greatest. The profit-maximizing level of output can also be determined by equating marginal revenue and marginal cost, known as the first-order condition for profit maximization. The second-order condition is that the slope of marginal revenue curve is smaller than the slope of marginal cost curve. If the firm is losing money but continues to produce, these conditions make sure that the firm minimizes losses.

The lowest point of the average cost curve is the firm's breakeven point. At the breakeven point, the firm earns a normal rate of return, defined as the average rate of return on investment in all industries. Any point above the breakeven point, the firm earns economic profits. The lowest point of the average variable cost curve is the shutdown point. If the firm shuts down temporarily at the shutdown point, the amount of loss is equal to fixed cost. The loss is smaller than the fixed cost, if the price is higher than the shutdown level. The loss is greater than the fixed cost, if the price is lower than the shutdown level. The segment of the marginal cost curve on or above the average variable cost curve is the short-run supply curve of firms that operate under perfect competition.

Profit-maximizing firms operating under a completely elastic demand curve select price at a level that is equal to marginal cost. Marginal cost pricing is said to be economically efficient. When price is equal to marginal cost for a given product, the maximum price that consumers are willing to pay for the product is exactly equal to what the society has to forgo to produce the product. When there are spillover effects, price no longer measures marginal cost accurately.

Effects of a trade between sellers and buyers on a third party who is not part of the trade are called spillover effects or externalities. Spillover effects beneficial to society are called spillover benefits or external benefits. Spillover effects detrimental to society are called spillover costs or external costs. Spillover costs cause the costs of production and the product prices to be underestimated, and lead to an overconsumption of these products. Spillover benefits cause the costs of production and the product prices to be overestimated, and lead to an underconsumption of these products.

There are four different types of auction. In the English auction, the price of an item is successively raised until only one bidder remains. In the Dutch auction, the auction price starts very high and is reduced gradually until a person accepts the bid price. In the first sealed bid auction, the bidder who submits the lowest or the highest sealed bid wins at the bid price. In the second sealed bid auction, the bidder who submits the lowest or the highest sealed bid wins but at the second lowest or highest bid price. Bidders in the first sealed bid auction and the Dutch auction reveal their true reservation price. Bidders in the second sealed bid auction and the English auction do not have to reveal the true reservation price to win the bidding.

Endnote:

1. Theodore M. Bernstein, "Economics Meets the Grammarian," *Business Horizons*, 30 (January-February 1987) 51.
2. Paul Milgrom, "Auctions and Bidding: A Primer," Journal of Economic Perspectives, 3 (Summer 1989), 3-22.

Chapter 10

Social Issues of Monopoly Markets

Markets that are imperfectly competitive vary considerably with the degree of control that individual firms have over the determination of the market price. Depending on the degree of control, markets are divided into monopoly, oligopoly, and monopolistic competition.

One important characteristic common to all imperfectly competitive markets is that sellers individually as well as collectively affect the determination of the market price. Unlike sellers under perfect competition, sellers under imperfect competition are **price makers**. Instead of charging the price that is determined in the market, they charge the price that can give them the maximum profit.

Revenue Curves under Imperfect Competition

Firms operating under market conditions that are imperfectly competitive are faced with a normal-looking demand curve that has a downward slope to the right. A monopoly firm and other firms under oligopolistic and monopolistically competitive industries can adjust the price of their products for maximum profits. An increase in the price of their products does not come free, however. A price increase decreases the quantity of their products demanded, while a price decrease increases the quantity of their products demanded.

The average revenue curve by definition is always the same as the demand curve, regardless of whether markets are perfectly competitive or imperfectly competitive. The average revenue curve of firms under imperfect competition has a downward slope to the right. When the average revenue curve has a downward slope to the right, marginal revenue from the sale of one additional unit would not be equal to the average revenue, since sales of additional units are expected to lower the price and, thus, the average revenue.

It is quite easy to derive the marginal revenue curve from a given average revenue curve. Note that a linear average revenue function is

$$P = a - bQ \qquad\qquad (10\text{-}1)$$

In (10-1) the slope of the average revenue schedule is "-b". Total revenue function is obtained by multiplying Q to (10-1):

$$TR = PQ = aQ - bQ^2 \qquad\qquad (10\text{-}2)$$

Since the marginal revenue function is the first derivative of total revenue function,

$$MR = dTR/dQ = a - 2bQ \qquad (10\text{-}3)$$

The slope of the marginal revenue schedule is twice (at -2b) the slope of its corresponding average revenue schedule (at -b). In Figure 10-1, AC is the average revenue curve, point A is the price at which the quantity demanded is zero, and point C is the quantity demanded at the zero price. The marginal revenue curve AB is obtained when OC is bisected at point B, and points A and B are connected.

Monopoly

If there is only one person selling hamburgers, cutting hair, building homes, or writing romance novels, each of these persons will soon become a millionaire. A market in which one firm produces and supplies a product that has no close substitutes is called a **monopoly**. Monopoly is the opposite of perfect competition. The one firm that produces the product is called a monopoly, monopolist, or a monopoly firm.

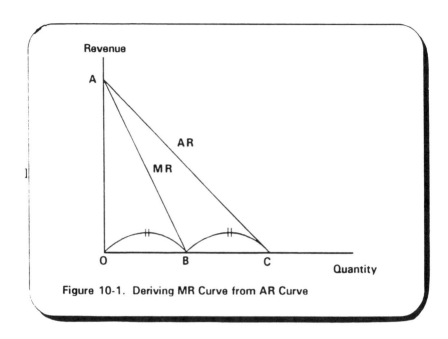

Figure 10-1. Deriving MR Curve from AR Curve

Utility Companies

Utility companies servicing the local market are often called monopolies. **Utility companies** are firms that supply public utilities such as electricity, natural gas, telephone, water, and sewer services. Strictly speaking, utility companies are not pure monopolies. Electric power companies compete with gas companies to attract customers, especially in the market for heating new homes under construction. The local telephone service has substitutes, albeit poor, in mail and messenger or delivery services. Tap water has a substitute in bottled water sold at supermarkets.

National Firms

When the scope of a market is defined in terms of the national market, examples of monopolies are harder to come by. Prior to World War II, for instance, the Aluminum Company of America (ALCOA) was the only predominant manufacturer of aluminum. Being the predominant producer of aluminum, ALCOA was a monopolist of aluminum, but was not a pure monopoly because it did have competition from producers of other metals that, to varying degrees, were substitutes for aluminum.

Although pure monopolies are rarely found, some companies have occasionally enjoyed market power so substantial that these companies were, for all practical purposes, pure monopolies. These companies included Western Electric, producing telephone equipment until the 1984 deregulation of American Telephone and Telegraph; IBM, whose market share for general purpose digital computer systems fluctuated around 80 percent in the 1960s and 1970s; and Xerox, with about 80 percent market share for electrostatic copier machines during the 1960s. Other products that reached monopoly status from time to time include nickel, magnesium, and Pullman railroad cars.

DeBeers is often cited as an example of a monopoly firm. The DeBeers diamond syndicate controls about 80 to 85 percent of the world's supply of diamonds. If the product is defined as precious stone instead of diamond, DeBeers is far from being a monopolist. There are numerous other precious stones such as emerald, sapphire, and opal.

Barriers to Entry

A monopoly firm can sustain monopoly power only if there are barriers to entry that prevent other firms from entering the same market. **Barriers to entry** are the factors that keep other firms from entering a given market. Barriers to entry provide potential monopoly firms with a source of monopoly power. Barriers to entry include ownership of an essential raw material, patents, economies of scale, government policies that impose barriers, and market imperfection.

Ownership of an Essential Raw Material

One major barrier to entry is the ownership or control of an essential raw material by the monopolist. The source of ALCOA's monopoly power before World War II was the control of bauxite, the key ingredient needed to produce aluminum. The source of DeBeers' monopoly power is the control of the diamond mines, especially in South Africa. Mergers of large companies are often triggered by the ownership of essential raw materials such as oil, coal, or platinum reserves by the company that is merged.

Patents

A **patent** is the exclusive right to produce a certain product or use a certain production technology. An interesting example that illustrates how a patent works to sustain monopoly power is the ballpoint pen. The ballpoint pen was invented by Milton Reynolds in 1945 and was patented by the Reynolds International Pen Company, which started production of the ballpen on October 6, 1945. The initial price was $12.50 when, in fact, the cost of production was estimated to be only 80 cents per pen.

A patent does not guarantee complete monopoly power, however. High economic profits by Reynolds prompted other competitors to enter the market with ballpoint pens that were similar, but not similar enough to violate patent laws. By December 1946 approximately 100 firms were making and selling ballpoint pens for as little as $2.98. By mid-1948 ballpoint pens were selling for as little as 39 cents and costing 10 cents to make.

A patent gives a firm temporary monopoly power and enables the firm to charge high prices, but sooner or later the free market disperses economic profits of the monopoly firm to later entrants to the market.

Economies of Scale

Economies of scale refer to cost advantages originating from large-scale operation. The so-called **heavy industries** such as the steel, automobile, and oil refinery industries, which require a large amount of expenditure on fixed inputs, are characterized by economies of scale. This means that larger firms can produce products at a lower unit cost than smaller firms. In industries characterized by economies of scale, firms that start on a small scale are not likely to survive because the small scale of operation results in a higher average cost of production. Economies of scale, therefore, effectively limit the number of potential entrants to the industry.

Government Imposition of Barriers

The government may legally allow certain firms to be monopolists. Examples of these firms are local water and sewer boards, local telephone services, and power and natural gas distributors. The reason for the government to allow public utilities to operate as legal monopolies is the requirement of a large expenditure on fixed inputs such as telephone poles, transmission cables, and water treatment plants. The hypothesis is that one firm can produce utilities at a lower unit cost than several smaller firms can. When one firm is allowed to supply the entire market, however, the lack of competition becomes a problem and the monopolist may be tempted to raise prices. For this reason, most states maintain agencies that regulate prices and other operating aspects of utility companies.

Pricing Behavior of Monopoly Firms

Monopoly firms determine price and the level of output in such a way as to maximize total profit. To find out how monopoly firms determine price and the level of output for maximum profits, we combine revenue curves and cost curves of monopoly firms as we did for firms operating under perfect competition. Cost conditions are essentially internal to the firm, so that the shapes of cost curves are the same for monopoly firms and competitive firms. What really makes the difference between monopoly firms and competitive firms is the difference in the market conditions under which these firms operate.

Stated simply, the firm operating under perfect competition is faced with competition from other firms in the same market that forces the firm to charge the market price, whereas monopoly firms are not faced with competition from other firms and, thus, can set their own price. The only constraint that the monopolist needs to consider in determining the product price is the law of demand. Higher prices will reduce the amount of sales, and lower prices will increase the amount of sales. The law of demand means that both the average revenue and marginal revenue curves for monopoly firms are sloped downward to the right.

The process for monopoly firms to make price and output decisions is shown in Figure 10-2. Figure 10-2 describes a monopolist operating at a breakeven point. Note that the MR = MC point lies directly below the breakeven point E at which the average cost curve (AC) is tangent to the average revenue schedule (AR).

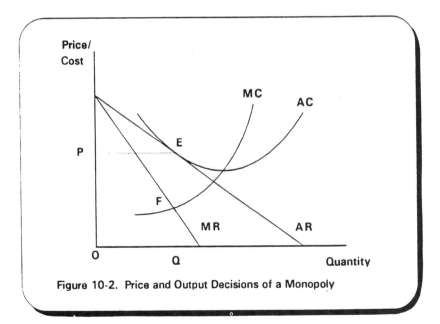

Figure 10-2. Price and Output Decisions of a Monopoly

We may generalize the pricing behavior of a monopolist in an algebraic form. Given the following total cost (TC) and demand (P) functions:

$$TC = TC(Q) \qquad\qquad (10\text{-}4)$$
$$P = P(Q); P'(Q) < 0 \qquad\qquad (10\text{-}5)$$

The first-order condition for profit maximization is derived from the profit (π) function

$$\pi = TR - TC$$
$$= QP(Q) - TC(Q) \qquad\qquad (10\text{-}6)$$

Taking the first derivative using the product rule of differentiation and setting it to zero for the first-order condition,

$$d\pi/dQ = QP'(Q) + P(Q)dQ/dQ - TC'(Q) \quad (10\text{-}7)$$
$$= QP'(Q) + P(Q) - TC'(Q) = 0 \qquad (10\text{-}8)$$

Solving for P

$$P(Q) = TC'(Q) - QP'(Q) \qquad\qquad (10\text{-}9)$$
$$= MC - QP'(Q)$$
$$= MC + MG \qquad\qquad (10\text{-}10)$$

in which MG stands for monopoly gain. The monopoly gain is positive because $P'(Q)$ is negative and thus the entire second term "$-QP'(Q)$" becomes positive. Under a perfectly competitive market, the monopoly gain becomes zero because the demand curve is horizontal and thus $P'(Q)$ becomes zero. When $P'(Q)$ is zero, the second term "$-QP'(Q)$" becomes zero. Unlike firms operating in perfect competition, the price is greater than the marginal cost for monopolistic firms.

Comparing Monopoly with Competitive Markets

Are competitive markets better than monopoly markets? To judge whether one is better or worse than the other, we need a basis on which to compare the two. In economics, the basis for comparing two different market structures is economic efficiency, also called allocative efficiency. If prices are lower and, as a result, the quantity of output traded is larger in market A than in market B, market A is said to be economically more efficient than market B.

The Hypothesis

In studies of market structure, one interesting hypothesis is that competitive markets are more efficient than monopoly markets. If this hypothesis were true, the price of a product would be lower and the quantity of the product traded would be larger under competitive markets than under monopoly markets. Our objective here is to find out whether competitive markets are, *ceteris paribus*, really more efficient than monopoly markets and, if they are, how much more efficient.

Graphic Illustration

Figure 10-3 is presented to clarify the basis for comparing the two market structures. In Figure 10-3, the average cost curve for individual firms of a given industry is drawn as a horizontal line based on the assumption that the average cost tends to vary little for a normal range of output. The average revenue curve in the figure is one for the industry and, thus, has a downward slope exhibiting the law of demand for both competitive and monopoly markets. Assuming that the market is competitive, firms earn no more than a normal rate of return, suggesting that the competitive price is equal to the average cost of production. At the competitive price P_c, the quantity demanded would be Q_c.

If the entire market is supplied by a monopolist, the monopolist will make decisions according to the MR = MC rule. Since the average cost curve (AC) is horizontal, the corresponding marginal cost curve (MC)

should be the same as the average cost curve. The monopolist charges
the monopoly price P_m, which is obtained by drawing a vertical line
from point B, at which marginal revenue equals marginal cost. The
monopoly price P_m is higher than the competitive price P_c. At the
monopoly price P_m, the quantity demanded would be Q_m, which is
smaller than the quantity demanded Q_c under a competitive market.
Figure 10-3 suggests, but does not necessarily prove, that competitive
markets are more efficient than monopolistic markets.

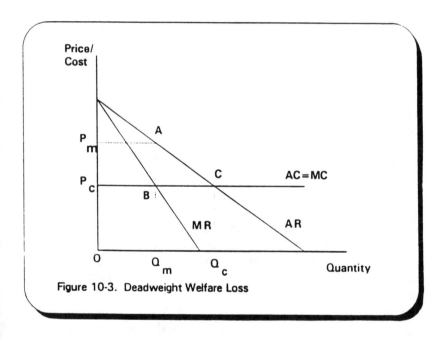

Figure 10-3. Deadweight Welfare Loss

The triangle ABC in Figure 10-3 represents a loss to society's welfare
by having a monopoly market as opposed to a competitive market. The

triangle ABC in Figure 10-3 is called the **deadweight welfare loss** (DWL). Deadweight means something that is lost permanently and not recoverable. Economic welfare is often measured in terms of the dollar value of goods and services consumed. The triangle ABC represents a loss in economic welfare, since the triangle represents the additional dollar value of products that consumers have to pay for having a monopoly market.

Empirical Studies of
the Deadweight Welfare Loss

What have economists found about the magnitude of the deadweight welfare loss? A substantial amount of deadweight welfare loss would indicate that society suffers substantially from allowing markets to be monopolistic. If this were the reality, it would make sense to promote competition in the economy. A small amount of deadweight welfare loss would indicate that we gain little from promoting competition in the economy.

After reviewing several studies which demonstrated that the welfare loss due to monopoly is small, R. A. Mundell suggests that unless there is a thorough theoretical re-examination of the validity of the tools by which these studies are founded, "someone inevitably will draw the conclusion that economics has ceased to be important!"[1] Like other empirical studies in economics, estimates of the deadweight welfare loss vary, although evidence points more toward a rather small loss. The welfare loss is typically presented as a percentage of national income. If the loss is 1 percent, for instance, the loss of income due to monopoly is 1 percent of the national income. An estimate by Arnold C. Harberger indicates that the loss is no more than 0.07 percent, while an estimate by D. Schwartzman is even lower, at 0.01 percent.[2] Critics of the Harberger study have calculated the welfare loss in the range of 4 to 6 percent.[3]

X-Efficiency

At least one economist hypothesizes that the amount to be gained from making the market more competitive and thus improving allocative efficiency is trivial, while the amount to be gained by increasing X-efficiency is significant.[4] **X-efficiency** is so called because the type of efficiency later defined as X- efficiency was initially undefined and was proposed for discussion purposes.

According to Professor Leibenstein, who proposed the hypothesis, the current operation of most, if not all, businesses is suboptimal regarding the use of technology, existing capital stock, and especially human resources belonging to these businesses. Leibenstein claims that "for a variety of reasons people and organizations normally work neither as hard nor as effectively as they could."[5] For instance, workers may come to work around 8 o'clock in the morning rather than by 8 o'clock, when they are supposed to start working. Also, the consideration of personal relations among workers sometimes keeps workers from being assigned to places where they are most efficient. The fact that firms are not as efficient as they could be in utilizing resources under their control is called **X-inefficiency**.

The main source of a firm's X-efficiency can be traced ultimately to managerial efficiency, since managers determine not only their own productivity but also the productivity of all cooperating units in the organization. A substantial reduction in unit costs can be realized when the X-efficiency of a firm improves. According to Leibenstein, the X-efficiency depends significantly on the degree of competitive pressure. The hypothesis of X- efficiency is another indictment against monopoly markets since the pressure needed to improve X-efficiency is greater in competitive markets than in monopolistic markets.

Natural Monopoly

A **natural monopoly** is a firm whose average cost of production declines over the entire range of market demand. Industries that are conducive to the creation of a natural monopoly are those in which the economies of scale are so large that the largest firm has the lowest per unit cost of production and is able to drive its smaller competitors out of the market. Natural monopoly is natural in that the declining long-run average cost gives an added advantage to the largest firm in the industry.

Problems with Natural Monopolies

When natural monopolies such as utility companies are allowed to become legal monopolies, there is a possibility that these companies may abuse the monopoly power. The monopoly power can be abused by providing services only to the point at which marginal revenue equals marginal cost, and charging the profit-maximizing price. To keep utility companies from charging the profit- maximizing price, all states maintain agencies that regulate the pricing behavior of utility companies.

There are many problems in regulation of public utilities. The problems include the determination of an optimal rate of return on investment in utility companies, the determination of an optimal price, identifying of all costs and revenues in a form that can be readily compared, and the determination of rates when, for instance, electricity is sold to neighboring states experiencing a temporary shortage.

Averch-Johnson Effect

State regulatory agencies generally use the fair rate of return approach by which utility companies are allowed to earn what the regulatory agencies consider to be the average rate of return on investment in plant and equipment. The rate base under the fair rate of return approach is the capital (plant and equipment) of utility companies. Under the fair rate of return approach, utility companies may be tempted to expand their plants and equipment, since the expanded capacity along with the current level of revenue will effectively lower the rate of return below the predetermined fair rate. To restore the fair return based on the expanded capacity, regulatory agencies will have to allow utility companies to raise utility rates.

The hypothesis that firms subject to rate of return regulation tend to overexpand their facilities is called the **Averch-Johnson effect**.[6]

Empirical studies that tested the Averch-Johnson effect show mixed results, however.

Contestable Markets

In presenting the theory of contestable markets at the 94th meeting of the American Economic Association, William J. Baumol, then president of the Association, said, "I must resist the temptation to describe the analysis I will report here as anything like a revolution."[7] The theory of contestable markets was advanced in several studies during the 1970s.[8] Policy implications of the theory are significant, especially when it is applied to markets characteristic of a natural monopoly.

Defining Contestable Markets

According to the **theory of contestable markets**, potential entry or competition for a monopolistic market disciplines the behavior of monopoly firms as effectively as actual competition would within the market. There are two key elements for market contestability. One is free entry and costless exit, and the other is the price flexibility that allows potential entrants to the market to undercut current suppliers. When these two conditions are met, markets are said to be contestable because of their vulnerability to hit-and-run operations by new firms in the industry. Contestable markets are readily subject to competitive forces, even when the markets are supplied by one or several firms. The number of sellers is not important according to the theory of contestable markets, because any economic profit in the industry will attract new entrants, which enter the market freely, charge prices below the level charged by existing firms, and exit the market costlessly as soon as economic profits disappear.

According to the theory of perfect competition, firms in an industry that is dominated by several large firms will no longer behave as price takers. Instead, these firms will charge a higher price and produce a lower quantity than they would under perfect competition. According to the theory of contestable markets, the existence of economies of scale is irrelevant so long as expenditures, known as sunk costs, on the large capacity of production are borne by an entity other than the firm itself. This point is crucial to understanding the usefulness of the theory of contestable markets, as shown in the following examples.

Examples of Contestable Markets

Consider the proposed merger between Texas International and National Airlines late in the 1970s.[9] The Houston-New Orleans market shares for the 12 months ending June 30, 1978, were 27 percent by National, 24 percent by Texas International, 23 percent by Delta, 17 percent by Continental, and 7 percent by Eastern. The U.S. Department of Justice opposed the merger based on the 51 percent market share of the two airlines if they were allowed to merge. The now-defunct Civil Aeronautics Board (CAB) recommended approval of the merger based on the theory of market contestability. In the airline industry, the largest sunk cost relates to the airport facility, owned by an entity such as the local airport authority that is independent of airline companies serving the area. Any new airline that plans to enter the Houston-New Orleans market will have to pay only a landing fee and rent for use of the airport terminal.

About a year later, a small regional carrier, Southwest Airlines, entered the market with a low-fare turnaround service and ended up offering about 25 percent of the capacity of the market. Proponents of the theory of contestable markets claim that the fast growth of Southwest Airlines supported the hypothesis that the Houston-New Orleans market was contestable.

Price Discrimination

Firms with monopoly power may discriminate prices for maximum profits. **Price discrimination** refers to charging different prices for the same product that are not justified by cost differences. Different prices may be charged to different buyers in different markets or to one buyer for different units of the same product.

Examples of Price Discrimination

Charging different prices to different buyers in different markets is quite common. Charges for local telephone service vary between commercial customers and residential customers. Charges for long distance telephone service are discriminated in favor of those who make calls in the evenings and weekends. Those who go to movies during the daytime are treated favorably with discount prices, while bus fares are often reduced for students and senior citizens. Examples thus far would not be a price discrimination if they are based on cost differences.

Psychiatrists are known to charge higher hourly fees for those with a higher income than for those with a lower income. Neighborhood dentists may charge higher fees for the same service to those who have dental insurance than to those without dental insurance. These practices are intended to increase profits by charging different prices to different consumers for the same service.

Requirements for Price Discrimination

If a firm is to succeed in increasing profits through price discrimination, three conditions have to be met. First, the firm has to have a monopoly power, since firms operating under competitive markets will be unable to change prices. Second, markets in which different prices are charged must be segmented with no possibility of resale among the segmented markets. Markets may be segmented in terms of location, time of day, income, age, sex, race, and so on. Third, consumers in segmented markets must be willing to pay different prices. Put differently, consumers in segmented markets must have different price elasticities of demand for the identical product. .

If, for instance, a person feels that his or her mental depression is serious enough to require counseling by a psychiatrist, but if the person is financially poor, the psychiatrist will have to lower the fee to have the poor person as a paying patient. If the person is wealthy, the psychiatrist can charge a high fee and still have the person as a paying patient. The price elasticity of demand for psychiatric services is high for the poor but low for the rich.

Summary

In monopoly, one firm produces and supplies a product that has no close substitutes. A monopoly firm is faced with a declining average revenue curve. When the average revenue schedule has a downward slope to the right, the slope of the marginal revenue schedule is twice the slope of its corresponding average revenue schedule. A monopoly firm can sustain monopoly power only if there are barriers to entry that prevent other firms from entering the same market. Barriers to entry include ownership of an essential raw material, patents, economies of scale, government policies that impose barriers, and market imperfection.   If prices are lower and, as a result, the quantity of output traded is larger in market A than in market B, market A is said to be economically more efficient than market B. One interesting hypothesis on market structure is that competitive markets are more efficient than monopoly markets. A comparison designed to test this hypothesis is graphed as a triangle representing the deadweight welfare loss. Deadweight means something that is lost permanently and not recoverable. Although not unanimous, empirical studies indicate that the deadweight welfare loss in the U.S. economy is rather small.

According the X-efficiency hypothesis, gains from making the market more competitive are trivial in comparison to gains from increasing X-efficiency. The fact that firms are not as efficient as they could be in utilizing resources under their control is called X-inefficiency. The main source of a firm's X-efficiency can be traced ultimately to managerial efficiency, since managers determine not only their own productivity but also the productivity of all cooperating units in the organization.

A natural monopoly is a firm whose average cost of production declines over the entire range of market demand. Utility companies are natural monopolies. State regulatory agencies of utility companies often use the fair rate of return approach by which utility companies are allowed to earn what the regulatory agencies consider to be the average rate of return on investment in plant and equipment. The hypothesis that this approach in rate regulation tends to lead utility companies to overexpand their facilities is called the Averch-Johnson effect.

When potential entry or competition for a monopolistic market disciplines the behavior of monopoly firms as effectively as actual competition would within the market, contestable markets are said to exist. There are two elements for market contestability; free entry and exit, and pricing flexibility. The theory of contestable markets was used as the basis for deregulation of industries.

Price discrimination refers to charging different prices for the same product that are not justified by cost differences. Different prices may be charged to different buyers in different markets or to one buyer for different units of the same product. Requirements for a successful price discrimination are monopoly power of a firm, market segmentation, and different price elasticities of demand among segmented markets.

Endnotes

1. R. A. Mundell, "Free Trade, Protection, and Customs Union," *American Economic Review*, 50 (June 1962), p. 622.
2 Arnold C. Harberger, "Monopoly and Resource Allocation," *American Economic Review*, 44 (May 1954) 77-87; D. Swartzman, "The Burden of Monopoly," *Journal of Political Economy*, 68 (December 1960) 727-729.
3. David R. Kamerschen, "An Estimation of the 'Welfare Losses' from Monopoly in the American Economy," *Western Economic Journal*, 4 (Summer 1966) 221-236.
4. Harvey Leibenstein, "Allocative Efficiency vs. "X-efficiency," *American Economic Review*, 56 (June 1966) 392-415.
5. Leibenstein, *Ibid.*, p. 413.
6. H. Averch and L. Johnson, "Behavior of the Firm under

Regulatory Constraint," *American Economic Review*, 52 (December 1962) 1052-1069.

7. William J. Baumol, "Contestable Markets: An Uprising in the Theory of Industrial Structure," *American Economic Review*, 72 (March 1982) 1-15; the quotation is from page 1.

8. Besides Baumol's article in *American Economic Review*, see Elizabeth E. Bailey, "Contestability and the Design of Regulatory and Antitrust Policy," *American Economic Review*, 71 (May 1981) 178-183; and Michael Spence, "Contestable Markets and the Theory of Industry Structure: A Review Article," *Journal of Economic Literature*, 21 (September 1983) 981-990.

9. This example is based on Bailey, "Contestability and the Design of Regulatory and Antitrust Policy," p. 181.

Chapter 11

Price and Output Decisions of Firms in Reality

Real markets are neither perfectly competitive nor purely monopolistic. In practically all industries, there is more than one producer of a product, but the number of firms is not large enough to make all firms price takers. Most real markets lie between perfect competition at one extreme and monopoly at the other. Economists classify markets between the two extremes into monopolistic competition and oligopoly.

Monopolistic Competition

Pharmaceutical companies that develop new brand-name drugs are called innovator drug companies. Innovator drug companies spend a large sum of money to develop a drug. When new drug is tested and finally approved by the Food and Drug Administration (FDA) for public use, the company gives it a brand name as Hoffmann-LaRoche did when it gave the name Valium to diazepam, a tranquilizer it developed. The innovator acquires a patent and becomes the only producer of the drug for the duration of the patent.

When the patent expires, any pharmaceutical company can apply for approval by the FDA to make its own version of the drug and market it under the drug's generic name, such as diazepam rather than Valium. This means that innovator drug companies make many generic drugs as well as all brand-name drugs. In fact, about 80 percent of generic drugs are manufactured by approximately 60 brand-name drug companies, and the remaining 20 percent are manufactured by about 300 smaller drug companies. Generic diazepam, for instance, is produced by more than a dozen companies to compete with Hoffmann-LaRoche's Valium.[1]

The main competition to brand-name drugs comes from smaller companies that produce generic drugs and charge lower prices for them. Generic drugs are expected to work as effectively as brand-name drugs because generic drugs must pass a bioequivalence test before the FDA will grant approval for production. Because manufacturers of brand-name drugs promote them heavily, brand-name drugs are priced substantially higher than generic drugs.

Why are consumers willing to pay a higher price for brand names? It is because consumers differentiate brand-name drugs from generic drugs, perceiving the brand-name items to be of a better quality, even if studies indicate that they are of equal quality. So long as consumers perceive brand-name drugs to be superior to generic drugs, manufacturers of brand-name drugs can charge higher prices for their products than can those who manufacture generic versions of the same drugs.[2]

Monopolistic Competition Defined

Based on this illustration, we are now ready for a more precise definition of monopolistic competition. **Monopolistic competition** refers to markets or market conditions in which a large number of sellers produce and sell differentiated products. The production of prescription drugs is monopolistically competitive in that there are many drug manufacturers producing differentiated drugs. Notice that product differentiation alone does not characterize monopolistic competition. If differentiated products are sold by only a small number of sellers, the market is oligopolistic, not monopolistically competitive. Only if differentiated products are sold by many sellers is the market monopolistically competitive. Good examples of monopolistic competition include markets for men's and women's dresses, fur goods, toothpaste, and wood furniture.

Product Differentiation

Product differentiation means that consumers perceive two or more products satisfying the same wants to be different and thus prefer one to the other. If the consumer perceives the two or more products to be the same, these products are said to be homogeneous. Whether any two similar products are homogeneous or differentiated depends ultimately on individual consumers' perceptions of the products, although the dominant opinion in the market is often generalized to indicate whether the two products are differentiated or homogeneous.

There are over 400 brands of pure aspirin sold in the United States. This number does not include such painkillers as Tylenol, Advil, Bufferin, and Anacin. These pain killers are not pure aspirin. According to publications such as Consumer Reports, all standard aspirin tablets contain 5 grams per tablet of acetylsalicylic acid and are equally effective.

Through advertising, Bayer has convinced consumers that Bayer aspirin is superior to other brands. Bayer has succeeded in differentiating its product from other brands of pure aspirin. It is widely known that Bayer charges a higher price for the same quantity of aspirin while still enjoying the largest market share. If consumers believe that all brands of pure aspirin are equally effective, aspirin is not differentiated to these consumers.

Another example of product differentiation relates to microbrewery. In the United States, approximately 90 percent of the beer market is controlled by the four largest brewers such as Anheuser-Busch, Miller, Coors, and Stroh is approximately 90 percent. Surviving among the giants are hundreds of microbreweries, comprising nearly 1.5 percent of the market share. The modern microbreweries started in 1976 in Sonosa, California, owing to the complaints by beer lovers that beers produced on a large scale do not meet their regional taste standards. Many beer lovers prefer a richer beer. Production of a rich beer is highly labor intensive, providing a comparative advantage to small breweries.

The basic equipment for a microbrewery can be purchased for about

$25,000 per 500 gallon system that includes a fermentation tank, a mixing tank, and a holding tank. Basic ingredients that includes malt, hops, yeast, and water are combined in the fermentation tank. The combination is as varied as the imagination of the braumeister who mixes them. The darker the roast of the malt, the darker and richer the beer is. Fermentation can take anywhere from three days to three weeks, depending on the temperature and the type of beer being made. The process is all controlled by braumeisters, who are known to have "the ego of an artist." The beer is the braumeister's until he or she releases it to be sold.

Monopolistic Competition in Graph

Figure 11-1 illustrates a monopolistically competitive firm that is breaking even. Figure 11-1 applies to all firms operating under market conditions that are imperfectly competitive. To suggest that there is a larger number of sellers in monopolistic competition than in monopoly or oligopoly, the average revenue curve is drawn closer to being horizontal. Figures 10-2 and 11-1 are identical except that the average revenue curve is more horizontal in Figure 11-1 for monopolistic competition than in Figure 10-2 for monopoly.

The firm depicted in Figure 11-1 is breaking even, since the average revenue curve is tangent at point E to the average cost curve. As usual, the firm is producing the quantity of output at OQ at which marginal revenue is equal to marginal cost, and charge the price indicated as OP, obtained by extending a line passing point E to the average revenue curve. It is important to draw marginal revenue and marginal cost curves in such a way that the intersection F between the two curves lies directly below point E.

Issues of Monopolistic Competition

Two issues relating to monopolistic competition merit further discussion: nonprice competition and social welfare implications.

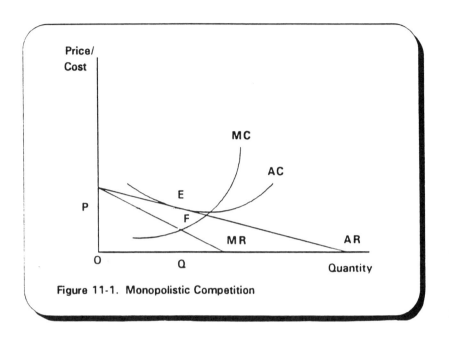

Figure 11-1. Monopolistic Competition

Nonprice Competition

Broadly speaking, firms employ nonprice competition to differentiate their products from products produced by their competitors. Nonprice competition involves two approaches: a promotion policy and a product policy. Both approaches are called nonprice competition because firms compete through means other than lowering the price of the product.

The promotion policy of firms refers to public announcements such as advertising intended to persuade consumers to buy their products. Advertisements by firms are usually more *persuasive* than *informative* and are intended to attract more customers. Advertisements by government or other nonprofit agencies are usually more informative than persuasive.

The product policy of firms refers to changes in the product such as an improvement of the product's quality, new and more attractive packaging, or an improvement in the delivery of services, that are intended to persuade consumers to buy their products.

Product Differentiation and Consumer Welfare

An interesting question relating to product differentiation is whether or not product differentiation through such means of nonprice competition as advertising is desirable from society's viewpoint. Product differentiation by its very definition suggests the availability of a large number of similar products that satisfy essentially the same want. Also, advertising may or may not increase the cost of production and subsequently the price of the product. It all depends on the extent of economies of scale that the additional output induced by advertising is subject to. Even if we assume that price is higher because of advertising, many people may still prefer the freedom of choice of having an option at the expense of higher prices. Car buyers would certainly prefer to have alternatives in the selection of new cars. No one who enjoys the freedom of choice will want to drive a Yugo, or even a Mercedes, all the time.

Oligopoly

An **oligopoly** is a market dominated by a small number of firms selling either homogeneous products or differentiated products. A market supplied by a large number of sellers is still an oligopoly if the market is dominated by a few large firms. Firms in an oligopolistic market recognize that their success depends not only on how well they run their own businesses individually, but also on how other firms respond to pricing and other promotional decisions that any one firm undertakes.

If firms under oligopolistic markets compete, their price and output decisions resemble those of firms operating under competitive markets. If they act in concert, their price and output decisions resemble those of monopolistic firms. Oligopolistic markets include the automobile, steel, aluminum, and cigarette industries. Two important characteristics of an oligopoly are mutual interdependence in pricing among oligopolists (the leading sellers), and barriers to entry into the industry.

Sellers in an oligopolistic market always consider possible responses from rival sellers in the industry when contemplating price changes or other promotional actions. Knowing that it is not easy for other firms to enter the industry, sellers in an oligopolistic market may not engage in highly competitive practices. The barriers to entry include patents that legally preclude other firms from producing the same product, consumers' brand loyalty toward existing products such as Coca Cola and the Lincoln Continental, and high capital costs needed to start a business in the oligopolistic industry, often characterized by economies of scale.

Kinked Demand Curve

The most widely known model of an oligopoly is the kinked demand curve, developed in the 1930s by Paul Sweezy.[3] According to the **kinked demand curve** hypothesis, price decreases of an oligopolist are matched by rival firms, but price increases are not matched. The kinked demand curve is shown in Figure 11-2.

The demand curve faced by an oligopolist is ABC in Figure 11-2 with a kink at point B. The AB portion of the demand curve explains the behavior of an oligopolistic firm that will not raise price, fearing that the price increase will not be matched by rival firms and will thus lead to a loss in sales. The BC portion of the demand curve explains the behavior of an oligopolistic firm that will not lower price, fearing that the price decrease will be matched by rival firms and thus nullify any advantage that the firm expects from lowering the price. The only rational pricing behavior of the oligopolistic firm then is to maintain the present price OP and sell the present quantity OQ. The hypothesis suggested by the kinked demand curve is that the price in an oligopolistic market tends to be rigid.

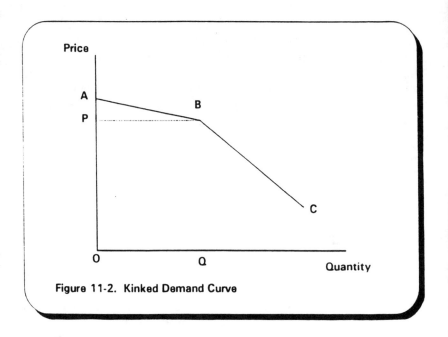

Figure 11-2. Kinked Demand Curve

Whether or not prices in oligopolistic markets are any more rigid than prices in other market structures is essentially an empirical question. If prices in oligopolistic markets are not any more rigid than prices in other markets, the kinked demand curve is simply an unsuccessful attempt to explain the pricing behavior of oligopolists. Some studies suggest that prices in oligopolies are no more rigid than prices in other markets.[4]

Another problem with the kinked demand curve is that the curve explains why prices in oligopolistic markets tend to be rigid but does not explain how the existing price level is determined. The kink on the kinked demand curve occurs at the existing price and sales level.

Because the kinked demand curve cannot explain how the existing prices and quantities of output are determined, the kinked demand curve hypothesis is not a model of price and output determination.

Price Leadership

Another way of explaining the mutual interdependence in pricing among firms operating under an oligopolistic market is price leadership. **Price leadership** refers to the practice in which one firm in the industry initiates a price change and other firms in the same industry follow the price leader by more or less matching the price change. Firms that lead the price change in oligopolistic markets are usually firms that can produce products at the lowest cost per unit. These firms tend also to be the most dominant firms in the industry. Price leaders in the recent past include U.S. Steel (now USX) in the steel industry, ALCOA in the aluminum industry, General Motors in the automobile industry, and R. J. Reynolds in the cigarette industry. When the dominant firm initiates a price change, the price leadership model hypothesizes that rival large firms and other small firms on the competitive fringe follow suit and change prices more or less proportionately.

Summary

In monopolistic competition, there are many sellers that sell differentiated products. Product differentiation means that consumers perceive two or more products satisfying the same wants to be different and thus prefer one to the other. When a product is differentiated, the demand for the product becomes less elastic and the firm producing the product is able to raise the price for greater total revenue. Product differentiation depends ultimately on the consumers' perception of the product.

Firms differentiate products through use of nonprice competition. There are two approaches to nonprice competition; a promotion policy such as advertising and a product policy such as improvements in the quality of the product or service. Product differentiation may or may not increase the cost of production and the product price, but provides more choices to the consumer.

In an oligopoly, a small number of firms sell either homogeneous products or differentiated products. A market supplied by a large number of sellers is still an oligopoly if the market is dominated by a few large firms. Oligopolistic markets are characterized by mutual interdependence in pricing and significant barriers to entry. The pricing behavior of oligopolists may be explained by the kinked demand hypothesis. According to the hypothesis, price decreases of an oligopolist are matched by rival firms, but price increases are not matched. The kinked demand hypothesis suggests that the price in an oligopolistic market is more rigid than in competitive markets. The kinked demand curve does not explain how the existing price level is determined. Another way of explaining the mutual interdependence in pricing among firms operating under an oligopolistic market is price leadership in which one firm in the industry initiates a price change and other firms in the same industry follow the price leader by more or less matching the price change.

Endnotes

1.   For more on generic and brand-name drugs, see "The Big Lie about Generic Drugs," *Consumer Reports*, 52 (August 1987) 480-485.
2.   The laws in all 50 states allow pharmacists to substitute a less expensive generic version when the doctor prescribes by brand, unless the prescribing doctor writes "dispense as written" or signs one of two lines dictating the prescription of brand-name drugs.
3.   Paul Sweezy, "Demand under Conditions of Oligopoly," *Journal of Political Economy*, 47 (August 1939) 568-573.
4.   For more on kinked demand curve, see George J. Stigler, "The Kinky Oligopoly Demand Curve and Rigid Prices," *Journal of Political Economy*, 55 (October 1947) 432-449; and Julian Simon, "A Further Test of the Kinky Oligopoly Demand Curve,"

American Economic Review, 59 (December 1969) 971-975.

Chapter 12

Market failures and Antitrust Laws

Suppose that a shortage of paper towels develops. In a competitive market, the shortage causes the price of paper towels to increase, signaling the shortage of the product. As the price of paper towels increases, existing firms will increase the quantity supplied of paper towels including Bounty, Job Squad, Viva, Brawny, and ScotTowels. New firms may also enter the industry, further increasing the supply of paper towels in the market. If a surplus develops, the opposite reaction will occur in the market. Most existing firms will reduce the quantity of the product they supply, while others will leave the industry.

Markets may not work as smoothly as they are described here, however. When price fails to signal shortages or surpluses of a product, the market fails to reallocate resources from one industry with surplus products to another industry experiencing a shortage of its product. **Market failure** occurs when price does not signal shortages and surpluses of a product in a given market. There are two popular examples of market failure, natural monopoly and externalities, discussed in order. The discussion of market failures is followed by a review of government regulation and antitrust laws.

Natural Monopoly

A **natural monopoly** is a firm that can supply the entire market demand on the declining portion of the firm's long-run average cost curve. Natural monopolies tend to develop in markets in which economies of scale are so large that the largest firm can supply the product to the entire market at the lowest cost per unit.

When a market is characterized by a natural monopoly, the largest firm will eventually be able to drive its smaller competitors out of the market. Once the monopoly status has been established, the natural monopoly will have the monopoly power to restrict output, raise prices, and earn monopoly profits. The government usually regulates that firm's rate of return on investment. Public utilities such as electricity, natural gas, water and sewer, and local telephone services are allowed to operate as a monopoly subject to state and local government regulation.

Externalities

To understand externalities, consider river water. No one owns the water. Since no one has property rights to the water, no one has control over its use. Water in fact is a free input into the production process. Without government regulation, firms will use river water as much as they can because it is free. This is how the market works, but the result is water pollution. Unfortunately, water pollution affects not only the firms that pollute the water, but the general public as well.

Defining Externalities

As discussed in Chapter 9, **externalities** refer to the effects of production on parties other than the immediate buyer and seller. If externalities benefit the third party, **external benefits** or **external economies** are said to exist. If externalities harm the third party, **external costs** or **external diseconomies** are said to exist. Externalities are also called **spillover effects**.

When there exist external costs such as water or air pollution, the supply curve of the product does not account for such costs incurred by society, and thus the market price tends to underestimate the social cost of production. **Social cost** measures the amount of other goods and services that society as a whole sacrifices to produce a given product.

Social cost includes both the firm's private cost of production and externalities. When external benefits exist, the demand curve of the product does not account for the benefits received by society, and thus the market price tends to underestimate the true value of the product.

Government has several options in dealing with the problem of externalities. For production of goods and services, such as flu shots, that benefit the general public, the government may provide a subsidy for research and development. The subsidy encourages production of these products by private firms that are not in a position to recover costs of producing the portion of benefits that accrues to the general public.

For goods and services whose production generates external diseconomies such as water or air pollution, the government may force firms to internalize the external costs through the levy of a pollution fee or direct regulation by the Environmental Protection Agency. In this case the government regulation causes the supply curve of the product to be shifted upward so that the supply curve can accurately measure the true costs of production to society. The government may also levy a tax on firms according to the amount of pollution that these firms emit and then use the tax revenue to clean up the pollution. In this case, the new tax also causes the supply curve of the product to be shifted upward and accurately measures the social cost of producing the product.

Theories of Government Regulation

Two theories are proposed to explain why government regulates the private sector of the economy. One is the public interest theory and the other is the capture theory.

Public Interest Theory

According to the **public interest theory of regulation**, government regulates industries in response to public demand for correction of market failures. To view the public interest theory in proper perspective, let us classify government regulation into two broad groups: economic regulation and social regulation. **Economic regulation**, also called **industrial regulation**, refers to government regulation of specific industries such as airlines, trucking, taxi service, railroad, community-antenna television (CATV) now called cable TV, and others. **Social regulation**, on the other hand, refers to government regulation across industries. In social regulation, government is concerned with issues such as safety and pollution that are common to many industries.

Richard A. Posner, of the University of Chicago Law School, reviewed a large number of studies on regulation and concluded that regulation was not positively correlated with the presence of monopolistic market structure.[1] If economic regulation is unrelated to the monopoly power of markets, economic regulation is not addressing the most important issue in government regulation, which is to make the market more competitive by reducing the monopoly power of firms. Posner claims that there is nothing intrinsic that requires government regulation in such industries as airlines, trucking, stock brokerage, ocean shipping, taxi service, and other heavy industries.

Capture Theory

According to the capture theory, government regulates industries not to protect public interest but to protect and promote the interests of the industries that are regulated.[2] The capture theory claims that government regulation is provided in response to the demand by firms in the regulated industry to maximize their profits. Regulatory services provided to firms in the regulated industries include price fixing, route fixing, restriction on entry through a license, and subsidies. Firms operating in a regulated industry are often protected from any cutthroat price competition or an erosion of market share by new entry into the industry.

Deregulation of Industries

Many government regulations began during the Great Depression years of the 1930s and continued to expand until the mid-1970s. Late in the 1970s, a forceful movement toward the deregulation of industries took place.

Perhaps the most important question concerning deregulation of industries is: Why bother? The answer is that we try to achieve through deregulation an improvement in economic efficiency. Specific objectives of deregulation are (1) lower prices and increased quantities of products traded, (2) improved quality of services, and (3) improved managerial efficiency. Following deregulation, we may anticipate a concentration of market shares to develop in the process of achieving these objectives. The concentration of market power may negate at least some advantages of deregulation.

Theoretical basis for the deregulation of industries is the theory of contestable markets, presented earlier in Chapter 10. The **theory of contestable markets** hypothesizes that firms in a highly concentrated market behave as if the market is competitive so long as the entry to and the exit from the market are costless. When markets are deregulated, a concentration of market share among a few firms is expected. According to the theory of contestable markets, the market concentration is not a problem so long as government ensures the free entry of new firms into and their free exit from the market.

Antitrust Laws

The term *trust* in antitrust means a combination of several corporations under the trusteeship of a single board of directors that manages these corporations jointly. Stockholders surrender their voting stock certificates in exchange for nonvoting trust certificates. Since profits are expected to be higher through the trust arrangement, the number of trusts grew rapidly in the late 1800s. Although the term antitrust was derived from the trust arrangement in the 1800s, the modern signification of the term is simply antimonopoly. Until 1890 there was no nationwide antitrust statute, and rulings on antitrust matters were based on common laws. Laws that deal with anticompetitive conduct and structure of firms are called **antitrust laws**.

Sherman Antitrust Act

The Sherman Antitrust Act was the first nationwide antitrust act in the United States. The Sherman Antitrust Act, named after the Ohio senator John Sherman who proposed it, was signed into law on July 12, 1890. The Sherman Antitrust Act is one of the shortest laws and contains eight brief sections, of which only the first two are substantive and the remaining describe more or less procedural matters.

Section 1 of the Act declared illegal any contract that restrained interstate trade, while Section 2 of the Act declared any attempt to monopolize a market illegal. The language of these two sections is straightforward, but what the law tried to say was far from clear. Regarding restraints of trade in Section 1, the Act did not clarify either what was and was not an interstate business or what specific acts constituted restraint of trade.

Regarding Section 2, the Act did not make clear whether it forbade certain types of business conduct only, or certain market structures as well as certain types of business conduct. For instance, the Act did not make clear whether the monopoly status of a firm that was obtained through internal efficiency and growth was illegal, as was the attempt to monopolize the market. The attempt to monopolize represents business *conduct*, whereas monopoly status represents a business *structure*.

Clayton Act

The Clayton Act, signed into law on October 15, 1914, was designed to correct the deficiency of the Sherman Act by spelling out behaviors of firms that constituted restraints of trade, and also by strengthening the powers of antitrust prosecutors. There are certain practices that the Clayton Act declared illegal, if their effects were to reduce competition substantially.

Section 2 of the Clayton Act prohibits price discrimination. Price discrimination based on differences in the cost of selling or transportation is not illegal. Section 3 prohibits **tying contracts**, which require a buyer to purchase unwanted products as a stipulation of the purchase of products that she does want, and **exclusive contracts**, which require the buyer not to deal with competitors of the seller. Section 7 prohibits monopolization through purchase of stocks of another company, if such an acquisition lessens competition substantially. Section 8 prohibits **interlocking directorates**, meaning that a person cannot be a director of two or more competing corporations. Section 8 has been largely unenforced.

There are a couple of other interesting sections in the Act. Section 4 allows private parties injured by violations of the Sherman and Clayton acts to sue for treble damages. If one can prove that the amount of the damage was $1 million, the award would be $3 million. Section 6 specifically exempts labor unions and agricultural organizations from the Sherman and Clayton acts.

It is interesting to note that the Clayton Act did not create criminal offenses. This means that the U.S. Department of Justice attorneys cannot bring charges under the Clayton Act, unless Sherman Act violations are also alleged. This explains in part why many of the alleged violations of antitrust laws are brought to court on the basis of both the Sherman Act and the Clayton Act.

Federal Trade Commission Act

The Federal Trade Commission (FTC) Act, signed into law on September 26, 1914, created the Federal Trade Commission and charged it with the exclusive authority to enforce Section 5 of the Act, stating that unfair methods of competition in or affecting commerce, and unfair or deceptive acts or practices in or affecting commerce, are unlawful. The exclusive authority to enforce means that private individuals have no standing to sue to enjoin violations of the FTC Act or to seek damages for such violations.

One of the interesting aspects of the FTC Act is the language of Section 5, which is so broad that it gives the FTC a semi-legislative authority to determine what methods of competition are undesirable.

Certain types of business conduct that do not necessarily violate antitrust laws may be judged unfair acts of competition by the FTC. The FTC holds hearings if law violations are suspected. If the FTC determines that a given business practice violates the FTC Act, it may either negotiate with the company to stop the practice, or initiate a legal procedure to force the company to cease and desist the practice.

Some past activities of the FTC include negotiations with automobile manufacturers to force correction of defects of automobiles for improved safety, and initiation and enforcement of the freedom by professionals such as doctors and lawyers to advertise their services.

Other Antitrust Acts

The major antitrust acts have been amended numerous times since their enactment.[3] When amendments are significant, these amendments carry their own names. Two of these significant amendments relate to the Clayton Act.

The 1936 amendment of Section 2 of the Clayton Act is known as the Robinson-Patman Act. Section 2 of the Clayton Act prohibits price discrimination. The Robinson-Patman Act was intended to protect small, independent wholesalers and retailers from large chain stores by prohibiting discounting to large buyers not justified by cost differences. The Robinson-Patman Act also prohibits discounting by a large seller among different localities if such discounting lessens competition substantially.

The 1952 amendment of Section 7 of the Clayton Act is known as the Celler-Kefauver Act. Section 7 of the Clayton Act prohibits purchase of stocks of another company for the purpose of monopolization. To avoid violation of the Clayton Act, firms had purchased plants and equipment, instead of stocks, for monopolization. The Celler-Kefauver Act closed this loophole of Section 7 by prohibiting the purchase of assets such as the plant and equipment of another firm for the purpose of monopolization. Section 7 prohibits stock acquisitions, whereas its 1952 amendment prohibits asset acquisitions, if such acquisitions reduce competition substantially.

Antitrust Issues and Policy

Antitrust laws are designed to achieve certain policy objectives. We discuss major policy objectives of antitrust laws in this section.

Intrastate or Interstate Commerce

When a business practice allegedly violating antitrust laws is tried under federal antitrust statutes, the practice must be judged to be interstate in nature rather than intrastate. If the practice is judged as intrastate commerce, it should be tried under state laws, not federal laws. Sometimes it is not easy to make a clear distinction between intrastate commerce and interstate commerce. Court rulings on whether any commerce is intrastate or interstate are usually based on the substantial effect doctrine. The **substantial effect doctrine** holds that any intrastate business practice exerting a substantial economic impact on interstate commerce falls under federal regulatory power.[4]

The trend is that more activities that appear local in nature have been ruled as being interstate. For example, in Oglesby and Barclift, Inc. v. Metro MLS, Inc., one of the early cases involving local real estate brokerage services, the court held that fixing a minimum commission and the percentage split of commissions by Metro MLS, Inc., violated the Sherman Act.[5] The ruling was based on the facts (1) that about 25 to 30 percent of home financing had been insured under VA and FHA programs, (2) that the members of Metro MLS advertised beyond the state line, and (3) that many members of Metro belonged to national referral organizations located outside the state.[6]

Monopolization

Section 2 of the Sherman Act forbids the act of monopolization. Main issues of monopolization relate to definitions of market share and relevant market. Courts typically use market share as a measure of monopoly power. In the ALCOA case, for instance, Judge Hand held that a 90 percent market share was sufficient to constitute monopoly power, but 60 percent would be insufficient.[7]

The main problem with the use of market share as a measure of monopoly power is that the concept does not take into consideration either the availability of substitutes or the contestability of the market, which measures how easy it is for new firms to enter the industry.

Defining a relevant market is a problem, also. For instance, the cellophane market may be defined broadly as one for flexible wrapping material rather than as one for cellophane wrapping material.[8] Or, professional championship boxing matches may be judged to constitute a market that is distinct from professional boxing matches in general.[9] There is no general rule beyond that commodities reasonably interchangeable by consumers for the same purposes make up the same trade. What is meant by reasonably interchangeable is subject to court interpretation.[10]

Mergers

A **merger** refers to the purchase of assets of a firm by another firm such that the two firms can be operated under one ownership. There are three types of mergers: horizontal, vertical, and conglomerate. A **horizontal merger** is a merger between two firms selling the same or similar products in the same market. A **vertical merger** is a merger between two firms that are related as supplier and buyer of a product. A **conglomerate merger** is a merger between two firms selling products that are unrelated.

Firms attempting a merger may consult merger guidelines prepared by the U.S. Department of Justice. The original guidelines were published in 1968 in order to determine whether or not to challenge corporate acquisitions and mergers. Revised guidelines were released by the Department of Justice on June 14, 1982. The revised guidelines are concerned more with market concentration and the likelihood of successful collusion among firms in a given market than with the overall size of the companies attempting a merger.[11]

Price Fixing

The Supreme Court ruled in the Socony Vacuum case that price fixing was illegal regardless of whether or not it served a worthy end, thus overwhelming any conceivable defense.[12] This means that price fixing is a *per se* (meaning "in itself" or "by definition") violation of the Sherman Act, and admits no defense or justification of any kind.

Fixing minimum prices among sellers and fixing maximum prices during an inflationary period for the benefit of consumers are both illegal. Also illegal is any agreement among competitors to limit production, although no specific fixed price is agreed upon. Price fixing applies not only to sellers but also to buyers. An agreement among buyers to offer a particular price or to limit purchases is illegal.

Although price fixing, if proven to have occurred, is an automatic violation of the Sherman Act regardless of the reasons for its occurring, proving price fixing is not an easy task. In this day and age, no one can be so naive as to believe that a formally signed and sealed contract or a written resolution would conceivably be adopted at a meeting of price fixing conspirators.[13] A typical price fixing agreement may be achieved through conscious parallel action. **Conscious parallelism** is a legal term meaning that an unlawful conspiracy to fix prices can be inferred in the absence of an explicit agreement if there is evidence that conduct stemmed from a tacit agreement.

Price Discrimination

Another important antitrust policy relates to price discrimination. According to the Robinson-Patman Act, it is illegal for any person to discriminate prices among different buyers of commodities of like quality where the effect is to reduce or prevent competition substantially.

Some interesting aspects of price discrimination are the following. First, both the seller who offers, and the preferred buyer who knowingly receives, discriminatory prices are guilty. Second, suppose that a product is produced in Paducah, Kentucky, and that the price of the product is the same all over the country. Such a uniform delivered price system may be judged illegal if buyers near Paducah are forced to pay **phantom freight**, the costs for freight that does not exist. Third, basing point prices may also be illegal if these prices contain phantom freight costs. According to the **basing point pricing system**, a firm selects one or more basing points or delivery points, and the delivered price is quoted as the product price at the nearest basing point, plus transportation cost.

The product price at the basing point is called an FOB (free on board) price, and the buyer is responsible for transportation cost. Phantom freights incur when the actual delivery of the product is made from a plant other than the basing point. Suppose a buyer in St. Louis buys a product that has a basing point in Kansas City. If the product is shipped from Kansas City to St. Louis and the delivered price is the FOB Kansas price plus transportation cost, there is no violation of the Robinson-Patman Act. If, however, the product is actually delivered from the company's warehouse in St. Louis, the basing point pricing system enables the firm to charge phantom freight from Kansas City to St. Louis, thus violating the Robinson-Patman Act.

Discriminatory prices do not violate the antitrust law if the differences in prices are based on (a) cost differentials, (b) meeting competition in good faith, or (c) changing conditions affecting the market or the marketability of goods such as deterioration of perishable goods, obsolescence of seasonal goods, or distress sales under court order or due to business closings.

Summary

Markets are said to fail when price does not signal shortages and surpluses of a product. Market failures may be caused by natural monopoly and externalities. A natural monopoly is a firm that can supply the entire market demand on the declining portion of the firm's long-run average cost curve. Externalities refer to the effects of production on parties other than the immediate buyer and seller. If externalities benefit the third party, external benefits or external economies are said to exist. If externalities harm the third party, external costs or external diseconomies are said to exist. When there exist external costs, the market price tends to underestimate the social cost of production. Social cost includes both the firm's private cost of production and externalities.

Two theories are proposed to explain why government regulates the private sector of the economy. According to the public interest theory of regulation, government regulates industries in response to public demand for correction of market failures. According to the capture theory, government regulates industries not to protect public interest but to protect and promote the interests of the industries that are regulated. Objectives of deregulation are lower prices and increased quantities of products traded, improved quality of services, and improved managerial efficiency.

Antitrust laws deal with anticompetitive conduct and structure of firms. The Sherman Antitrust Act, enacted in 1890, was the first nationwide antitrust act in the United States. Section 1 of the Act declared illegal any contract that restrained interstate trade, while Section 2 of the Act declared any attempt to monopolize a market illegal. The Clayton Act, signed in 1914, was designed to correct the deficiency of the Sherman Act. There are certain practices that the Clayton Act declared illegal, if their effects were to reduce competition substantially. These practices include tying contract, exclusive contract, purchase of stocks for monopolization purposes, and interlocking directorates. The Clayton Act also allows treble damages for a successful litigation in antitrust cases. Unlike the Sherman Act, the Clayton Act did not create criminal offenses. This explains why many of the alleged violations of antitrust laws are brought to court on the basis of both the Sherman Act and the Clayton Act.

The Federal Trade Commission (FTC) Act, enacted in 1914, created the Federal Trade Commission and charged it with the exclusive authority to reduce unfair competition. Some past activities of the FTC include negotiations with automobile manufacturers to force correction of defects of automobiles for improved safety, and initiation and enforcement of the freedom by professionals such as doctors and lawyers to advertise their services.

The 1936 amendment of Section 2 of the Clayton Act is known as the Robinson-Patman Act. The Robinson-Patman Act was intended to protect small, independent wholesalers and retailers from large chain stores by prohibiting discounting to large buyers not justified by cost differences. The 1952 amendment of Section 7 of the Clayton Act is known as the Celler-Kefauver Act. This Act closed the loophole of the Clayton Act by prohibiting the purchase of assets such as the plant and equipment of another firm for the purpose of monopolization. Section 7 of the Clayton Act prohibits stock acquisitions only.

According to the substantial effect doctrine, any intrastate business practice exerting a substantial economic impact on interstate commerce falls under federal regulatory power. More activities that appear local in nature have been ruled as being interstate. A merger refers to the purchase of assets of a firm by another firm such that the two firms can be operated under one ownership. There are three types of mergers: horizontal, vertical, and conglomerate. Firms attempting a merger may consult merger guidelines prepared by the U.S. Department of Justice. Price fixing is a *per se* violation of the Sherman Act; it is illegal regardless of whether or not it served a worthy end. The basing point pricing system may lead to phantom freight by charging a freight from one of basing points when in fact the product is delivered from a local warehouse. Phantom freights may constitute price discrimination. In price discrimination, both the seller who offers, and the preferred buyer who knowingly receives discriminatory prices, are guilty.

Endnotes

1.   Richard A. Posner, "Theories of Economic Regulation," *Bell Journal of Economics and Management Science*, 5 (Autumn 1974) 335-358.

2.   For the capture theory, see George J. Stigler, "The Theory of Economic Regulation," *Bell Journal of Economics and Management Science*, 2 (Spring 1971) 3-21, and Sam Peltzman, "Toward a More General Theory of Regulation," *Journal of Law*

and Economics, 19 (August 1976) 211-240.

3. *Antitrust Laws with Amendments 1890-1970*, (Washington, D.C.: U.S. Government Printing Office, 1971).

4. *Wickard v. Filburn*, 317 U.S. 111 (1942).

5. *Oglesby & Barclift, Inc. v. Metro MLS, Inc.*, 1976-2 CCH Trade Cases No. 61,064.

6. For more on the difference between intrastate and interstate commerce and other antitrust issues of multiple listing services, see Semoon Chang, "Multiple Listing Services: The Antitrust Issues," *Real Estate Law Journal*, 10 (Winter 1982) 228-246.

7. *U.S. v. Aluminum Co.*, 148 F.2d 416, 424. In the United Shoe case, on the other hand, Judge Wyzanski held that a 75 percent market share was sufficient. *U.S. v. United Shoe Machinery Corp.*, 110 F.Supp. 295.

8. *U.S. v. E. I. duPont*, 351 U.S. 377, 1956.

9. *Boxing Club v. U.S.*, 358 U.S. 242, 1959.

10. *U.S. v. E. I. duPont*, 351 U.S. 377, 1956.

11. References on merger guidelines include Merger guidelines of the Department of Justice, *Trade Regulation Reporter*, Commerce Clearing House, Paragraph 4510 (1980); Albert A. Foer, "The New Antitrust Guidelines: Full Speed Ahead for Business Combinations," *Business and Society Review*, 44 (Winter 1983) 23-28; and Joseph E. Gagnon, "The New Merger Guidelines: Implications for New England Banking Markets," *New England Economic Review*, (July-August 1982) pp. 18-26.

12. *United States v. Socony-Vacuum Oil Co.*, 310 U.S. 150 (1940).

13. *Esco Corp. v. United States*, 340 F.2d 1000 (9th Cir. 1965).

Chapter 13

Forecasting Methods and Techniques

In a market economy, where decisions on production of goods and services are made by individual producers, the total demand for goods and services in the economy, known as aggregate demand, will not always match their total supply called aggregate supply. Fluctuations in business activities are unavoidable.

Why Need Forecasts?

In macroeconomic forecasting, we try to predict likely future values of major economic variables. Major economic variables that are regularly forecast by professional forecasters include nominal gross domestic product (GDP), real GDP, components of nominal and real GDP, consumer price index (CPI), labor force, employment, unemployment, the rate of unemployment, and sales of major manufactured products such as automobiles. Since most economic variables tend to move together with fluctuations in real GDP, greater attention is paid to forecasting real GDP.

If we can accurately forecast future fluctuations in the economy subject to existing policy constraints, we will be able to minimize the magnitude of the fluctuation and, thus, minimize economic losses. If we know, for instance, that the economy for the next two years is not likely to grow so long as current policies continue, the government may undertake expansionary economic policies to promote additional business activities. If we know that the economy is not expected to grow, private businesses may prepare for the slowdown by reducing their production and tightening inventories.

In this situation, the actions of private businesses may worsen, or even cause, the downturn even though the forecast would otherwise have been erroneous. If the economy is not expected to grow, public officials of the local government may expect a slow increase in, if not a decrease in, tax revenues and become cautious about hiring additional police officers or garbagemen.

There are many firms that specialize in forecasting business and economic variables. Well known among these firms are DRI/McGraw-Hill in Lexington, Massachusetts, which enjoys hundreds of corporate customers, Wharton EFA in Philadelphia, and Chase Econometrics in New York. Most business magazines routinely carry forecasts of major economic variables made by leading forecasters, although forecasts of specific variables are available only to their paid subscribers. Readers may subscribe Blue Chip Economic Indicators of Capitol Publications, a monthly summary of U.S. economic forecasts made by many different professionals.

These days, most professional forecasters employ econometric methods. **Econometric methods** are statistical methods applied to theoretical models of economic reality. The most powerful statistical method applied to economic forecasting is the regression analysis (presented in Chapters 4 and 5), which postulates a causal relation between a dependent variable such as real GDP and one or more independent variables such as business investment and interest rates. Regardless of which econometric equations individual forecasting firms use, professional forecasters all watch changes in the composite index of leading indicators.

Before we study the basics of econometric forecasting, let us review the history of macroeconomic theories, since today's econometric forecasting models for the U.S. economy have their roots in macroeconomic theories.

Classical Economics

Classical economics is the collection of economic ideas that were developed between 1776 and 1870 by such social scientists as Adam Smith (1723-1791), Thomas R. Malthus (1766-1834), Jean Baptiste Say (1767-1832), David Ricardo (1772-1823), and John Stuart Mill (1806-1873). A general consensus regards the beginning of the classical economics as 1776, when Smith published the *Wealth of Nations*.[1] The classical school may have ended in 1870, but the main ideas of classical economics were not seriously challenged until 1936, when John Maynard Keynes published his *General Theory*. The classical economic ideas, summarized in the below, are very much alive today, and will be so for many years to come.

Economic Philosophy

The period from 1750 to 1850 is often used to date the industrial revolution in Europe, and England was the first nation that experienced an industrial revolution. By 1750, however, England was ahead of other countries, aided by inventions of machines in the cotton textile industry, inventions in metals and machine tools, and inventions to provide power to drive the machines. By 1776 England became one of the most efficient and powerful countries in the world. As English entrepreneurs became stronger, they wanted free trade without fear of foreign competition.

The economic philosophy of classical economics was **laissez faire**. According to this view, the best government is one that governs least. The forces of the free, competitive market guide production, exchange, and distribution. Each person, if left alone, will seek to maximize his or her own wealth. By seeking his or her own interests, each individual serves the best interests of society. There exists an invisible hand that harmonizes the self-interests of individual producers and consumers for the benefit of society. Through the **invisible hand**, the attempt by each person to maximize his or her own wealth also maximizes the nation's wealth. The invisible hand is equivalent, in modern terms, to the demand and supply mechanism of the competitive market.

Labor Market

Money wages are flexible; they can rise or fall. Wages rise when the demand for workers is greater than the supply of workers. Wages fall when the supply of workers is greater than the demand for workers. More precisely, wages rise when there is a shortage of workers until the shortage no longer exists; and wages fall when there is unemployment until all unemployed persons find work at prevailing wages. Because wages are flexible, unemployed workers are all **voluntarily unemployed**. Workers are unemployed because they refuse to work at prevailing wages. There is no involuntary unemployment.

Output Market

According to classical economics, prices are flexible, rising and falling. If there is a shortage of a product, the price of the product rises, causing the quantity of the product supplied to increase and the quantity of the product demanded to decrease. If there is a surplus of a product, the price of the product falls, causing the quantity of the product supplied to decrease and the quantity of the product demanded to increase. In either case, the flexibility of prices assures that shortages and surpluses are only temporary phenomena.

To generalize, the supply of a product creates its own demand through changes in prices. Since the quantity of output supplied equals the quantity of output demanded, the economy is in equilibrium. The equality between saving and investment only reinforces this process toward equilibrium. The hypothesis that supply creates its own demand is known as **Say's law**, named after Jean Baptiste Say, a French economist who popularized Adam Smith's ideas on the European continent.

Money and Prices

According to classical economics, the general level of prices in the economy depends directly on the quantity of money circulating in the economy. Put differently, the quantity of money circulating in the economy determines the general level of prices. The greater the money supply, the faster prices increase. The causal hypothesis between the supply of money and the general level of prices is known as the **quantity theory of money**.

From Classical to Keynesian Economics

On Black Thursday, October 24, 1929, the stock market collapsed, signaling the beginning of the Great Depression. The magnitude of the depression was overwhelming. The U.S. GNP in 1929 dollars was $104.4 billion in 1929, but decreased to $74.2 billion in 1933 and did not return to the 1929 level until 1937. The CPI with 1947-1949 as the base period was 73.3 in 1929, but decreased to 55.3 in 1933 and did not return to the 1929 level until the outbreak of World War II.

In 1933 the rate of unemployment reached 25 percent of the labor force, with over half of the labor force having been laid off at least once during the year. There was no social security, no food stamps, no Medicaid, and no aid to families with dependent children in 1933. The Dow Jones industrial average fell from 381 in 1929 to 41 in June 1932.

It was obvious that the depression shook the capitalistic economic system to its core. The *laissez faire* policy of classical economics was unable to correct the problem. It was about time for someone to come up with new ideas. Economic fluctuations in the United States since 1854 are summarized in Table 13-1.

Keynesian Economics

John Maynard Keynes is considered to be one of the greatest economists of all times. Keynesian economics is often referred to as the Keynesian revolution. Followers admire him; opponents belittle him. The basic ideas of **Keynesian economics** is reviewed below.

Table 13-1. Fluctuations of the U.S. Economy

Business Cycles Reference Dates		Duration (months)			
		Contract (Trough from Previous Peak)	Expansion (Trough to Peak)	Trough from Last Trough	Peak from Last Peak
Trough	Peak				
Dec. 1854	June 1857	-	30	-	-
Dec. 1858	Oct. 1860	18	22	48	40
June 1861	Apr. 1865	8	46	30	54
Dec. 1867	June 1869	32	18	78	50
Dec. 1870	Oct. 1873	18	34	36	52
Mar. 1879	Mar. 1882	65	36	99	101
May 1885	Mar. 1887	38	22	74	60
Apr. 1888	July 1890	13	27	35	40
May 1891	Jan. 1893	10	20	37	30
June 1894	Dec. 1895	17	18	37	35
June 1897	June 1899	18	24	36	42
Dec. 1900	Sep. 1902	18	21	42	39
Aug. 1904	May 1907	23	33	44	56
June 1908	Jan. 1910	13	19	46	32
Jan. 1912	Jan. 1913	24	12	43	36
Dec. 1914	Aug. 1918	23	44	35	67
Mar. 1919	Jan. 1920	7	10	51	17
July 1921	May 1923	18	22	28	40
July 1924	Oct. 1926	14	27	36	41
Nov. 1927	Aug. 1929	13	21	40	34
Mar. 1933	May 1937	43	50	64	93
June 1938	Feb. 1945	13	80	63	93
Oct. 1945	Nov. 1948	8	37	88	45
Oct. 1949	July 1953	11	45	48	56
May 1954	Aug. 1957	10	39	55	49
Apr. 1958	Apr. 1960	8	24	47	32
Feb. 1961	Dec. 1969	10	106	34	116
Nov. 1970	Nov. 1973	11	36	117	47
Mar. 1975	Jan. 1980	16	58	52	74
July 1980	July 1981	6	12	64	18
Nov. 1982	July 1990	16	93	28	109
Mar. 1991		7	-	101	-

Sources: National Bureau of Economic Research, Inc., as published in U.S. Department of Commerce Bureau of Economic Analysis, *Business Conditions Digest*, 23 (July 1983):103, and 28(March 1988):10, and *Survey of Current Business*, 73 (October 1993), C-7.

Economic Philosophy

Keynes felt that the classical *laissez faire* policy would not bring about a full employment economy. Keynes thus advocated government intervention in the private enterprise system. Keynes's economic philosophy was attacked from the left (liberal economists) and the right (conservative economists). Critics on the left accused him of being an apologist for capitalism, while critics on the right accused him of being a socialist who wanted to attack the capitalistic economic system. The truth is that Keynes supported capitalism and opposed totalitarian governments. He supported the individualism and freedom that were inherent in capitalism. He simply foresaw the need for an increased role of government in the capitalistic system.

The Keynesian vision was that the emphasis on saving in classical economics had outlived its usefulness in an environment that needed spending more than saving. The idea of stressing spending not only by consumers but especially by the government became the core of his new macroeconomic theory.

Labor Market

According to Keynes, money wages are flexible upward but not downward. Wages rise when the demand for workers is greater than the supply of workers. However, wages do not fall when the supply of workers is greater than the demand for workers. Wages increase when there is a shortage of workers, but stay the same when there is unemployment. The downward rigidity of wages is due to several factors, such as labor unions, minimum wage regulations, and tradition.

Because wages do not fall when unemployment exists, unemployed persons who are willing to work at prevailing wages or wages below the prevailing level cannot find work. In other words, unemployment that exists under the assumption of downwardly rigid wages is **involuntary unemployment**. Unemployed persons cannot find work at prevailing wages even if they want to work. Unemployment is no longer temporary, as classical economists believed it to be.

Output Market

Keynes assumes that, like wages, prices are also flexible upward but not downward. If there is a shortage of a product, the price of the product rises, causing the quantity of the product supplied to increase and the quantity of the product demanded to decrease. If there is a surplus of a product, however, the price of the product does not necessarily fall and the surplus continues. Because of the downward rigidity of prices, supply does not create its own demand through changes in prices. Keynes thus rejects Say's law, and claims that surplus output and unemployment may persist without government intervention. Even if Say's law is valid, the process of clearing the market is so time-consuming that full employment equilibrium may be forever pursued but never attained.

Money and Prices

Contrary to the classical economists' claim that changes in money supply affect prices but not the interest rate, Keynes claims that the major impact of changes in money supply is on the interest rate. An increase in money supply lowers the interest rate; a decrease in money supply raises the interest rate. Only if the money supply is increased in large amounts is the increase in money supply inflationary. Keynes does not support the quantity theory of money, at least in the short run. The long-run impact of changes in money supply was not the main concern in Keynesian economics.

Macroeconomic Forecasting

Econometric forecasting models for the U.S. economy may be based either on the classical economics or the Keynesian economics, depending on one's preference. In this section, we develop a simple forecasting model based on the Keynesian economics for the sole purpose of illustration.

Identity

In equilibrium, the aggregate supply (AS) of goods and services produced in an economy is equal to their aggregate demand (AD):

$$AS = AD \qquad (13\text{-}1)$$

According to Keynes, there are four components in aggregate demand; consumption demand (C), business investment demand (I), government demand (G), and the difference between exports (X) and imports (M). Since AS is gross domestic product Y, identity (13-1) may be restated as

$$Y = C + I + G + X - M \qquad (13\text{-}2)$$

If we want to use (13-2) to forecast the level of GDP for the next year, we need to know the values of C, I, G, and (X - M) for the next year. The problem is that at least some of these demand variables depend on the very value of Y for the next year that we are interested in forecasting. For instance, to forecast Y for next year, we need to know the value of C for next year. The value of C for next year, however, is not known without the knowledge of the value of Y for the next year.

Behavioral Equations

We need to examine all variables in the right side of (13-2). First, we transform C to a consumption function by assuming that consumption depends on disposable income (Y_d):

$$C = a + bY_d \qquad (13\text{-}3)$$

where disposable income is the difference between total income or output (Y) and taxes (T):

$$Y_d = Y - T \qquad (13\text{-}4)$$

$$T = c + dY \qquad\qquad (13\text{-}5)$$

Equation (13-3) is a Keynesian consumption function in which "a" is a y-intercept representing an autonomous consumption. "Autonomous" means that the value of "a" does not depend on the value of Y_d. Note that $C = a$ when $Y_d = 0$, meaning that even if there is no income, consumers will have to spend "a" perhaps to survive. In tax function (13-5), "c" represents taxes that are invariant to the income level and may include property taxes and import duties. The term dY represents taxes that vary with income, such as income and sales taxes.

Second, we assume that business investment (I) depends on the rate of interest (R), which in turn is set by the Federal Reserve Bank:

$$I = e - fR \qquad\qquad (13\text{-}6)$$
$$R = R^g \qquad\qquad (13\text{-}7)$$

Obviously, the assumption that the investment depends inversely on interest rates is too simple, and the assumption that interest rates are set by the Federal Reserve is not true. At least, equations (13-6) and (13-7) strongly suggest that there will have to be a great number of equations to specify a model if the model can describe the real economy.

Also, we cannot make all variables to depend on one another in a model. Somewhere, we have to draw a line by assuming that the values of certain variables should be given to the model from outside. These variables are called **exogenous variables** as opposed to **endogenous variables** whose values are determined within the model. In our simple model, we treat R (interest rate), G (government spending), and X (exports) as exogenous variables, in the sense that tax revenues of the federal government are predetermined in Congress and exports depend more on the economic health of other nations. Exogenous variables carry a superscript "g" to denote that their values are given *a priori*. That is,

$$G = G^g \qquad\qquad (13\text{-}8)$$
$$X = X^g \qquad\qquad (13\text{-}9)$$

Finally, imports (M) are assumed to depend on the level of our income (Y);

$$M = g + hY \qquad (13\text{-}10)$$

Solving the Model

Reconsider (13-2), and replace the four independent variables with behavioral equations specified in (13-3) through (13-10) as follows:

$$
\begin{aligned}
Y &= C + I + G + X - M \qquad (13\text{-}2) \\
&= a + bY_d + e - fR + G + X - (g + hY) \\
&= a + b(Y - T) + e - fR + G + X - (g + hY) \\
&= a + b(Y - (c + dY)) + e - fR^g + G^g + X^g - (g + hY)
\end{aligned}
$$
$$(13\text{-}11)$$

Expanding,

$$Y = a + bY - bc - bdY + e - fR^g + G^g + X^g - g - hY$$

Transferring all Y's to the left,

$$Y - bY + bdY + hY = a - bc + e - fR^g + G^g + X^g - g$$

Factoring out by Y in the left,

$$(1 - b + bd + h)Y = a - bc + e - fR^g + G^g + X^g - g$$

Dividing both sides by $(1 - b + bd + h)$, we obtain the solution

$$Y = [1/(1 - b + bd + h)][a - bc + e - fR^g + G^g + X^g - g]$$
$$(3\text{-}12)$$

The process of forecasting Y for the next year is as follows: First, estimate the values of all lower-cased letters in equation (3-12) through regression estimation of (13-3) for "a" and "b"; (13-5) for "c" and "d";

(13-6) for "e" and "f"; and (13-10) for "g" and "h". Second, we obtain the next year's values of all exogenous variables, R^g and X^g in our model. Finally, we plug all these values into (13-12) to obtain the next year's value of Y.

Equation (3-12) allows us to test how sensitive the value of Y is to changes in the value of exogenous variables. The process of this test is known as the **sensitivity analysis**. For example, if we want to see how changes in interest rate affect the GDP forecast, we replace the existing value of R^g with its new value and re-estimate (3-12) for new Y. The difference between the new value of Y and the value obtained from the old interest rate is the impact of the changes in the interest rate. In fact, the impact is

$$[1/(1 - b + bd + h)] \times \Delta R^g \qquad (13\text{-}13)$$

The term $[1/(1 - b + bd + h)]$ is the multiplier.

Composite Index of Leading Indicators

Many economists use economic "barometers" to forecast a change in business conditions. One barometer that is watched widely by economic forecasters and the business community is the composite index of leading indicators.

Cyclical Indicators

The recurring pattern of expansion and contraction of the overall activity of an economy is called the **business cycle**. Economists have long searched for an economic series that would give a signal of changes in economic activity that can be used to forecast business cycles.

The first serious attempt to select economic series as indicators to predict business cycles was made in the 1920s. The business cycle indicators were published by the Harvard Economic Service. This early system of indicators, called the Harvard ABC curves, was popular but was discontinued when it supposedly failed to predict the Great

Depression.

During the 1937-38 recession, U.S. Treasury Secretary Henry Morgenthau, Jr., asked the National Bureau of Economic Research (NBER) to develop a system of economic indicators that would signal the end of the recession. The NBER was, and still is, a private nonprofit research organization. Under the leadership of Wesley C. Mitchell and Arthur F. Burns, the NBER had collected and analyzed hundreds of economic series. Based on their analysis, Mitchell and Burns selected a number of series that appeared reliable in predicting past business recoveries.

There have been many modifications and refinements in the original list, published in May 1938 by the Treasury Department. A comprehensive review of cyclical indicators was conducted from 1972 to 1975 by the Bureau of Economic Analysis (BEA) of the U.S. Department of Commerce, with the cooperation of the NBER research staff. Data on cyclical indicators and indexes of cyclical indicators are published every month in Survey of Current Business by the U.S. Department of Commerce.

Economic series can be classified with respect to the reference dates of business cycle chronology of peaks and troughs. Series that historically reached their own cyclical peaks and troughs earlier than the corresponding turns in the business cycle are called **leading indicators**. Series that historically reached their own cyclical peaks and troughs at about the same time as the corresponding turns in the business cycle are called **coincident indicators**. Series that historically reached their cyclical peaks and troughs later than corresponding turns in the business cycle are called **lagging indicators**.

There are 108 cyclical indicators that are classified as leading indicators, 47 indicators that are classified as coincident indicators, and 60 indicators that are classified as lagging indicators. When news media mention leading, coincident, or lagging indicators, however, these indicators are usually composite indexes of indicators. The composite index of leading indicators comprises only 11 leading indicators; four coincident indicators make up the composite index of coincident indicators; and seven lagging indicators make up the composite index of lagging indicators. The components of the three composite indexes are listed in Table 13-2.

Table 13-2. Composite Index Components

Leading indicators

    Average weekly hours of production or nonsupervisory workers, manufacturing
    Average weekly initial claims for unemployment insurance, state programs, inverted
        scale
    Manufacturers' new orders in 1982 dollars, consumer goods and materials industries
    Vendor performance, slower deliveries diffusion index, percent
    Contracts and orders for plant and equipment in 1982 dollars
    Index of new private housing units authorized by local building permits, 1967 = 100
    Change in manufacturers' unfilled orders in 1982 dollars, durable goods industries,
        smoothed
    Change in sensitive materials prices, smoothed
    Index of stock prices, 500 common stocks, 1941-43 = 100
    Money supply M2 in 1982 dollars
    Consumer expectations, University of Michigan

Coincident indicators

    Employees on nonagricultural payrolls
    Personal income less transfer payments in 1987 dollars
    Manufacturing and trade sales in 1987 dollars
    Index of industrial production, 1987 = 100

Lagging indicators

    Average duration of unemployment in weeks, inverted scale
    Ratio, manufacturing and trade inventories to sales in 1982 dollars
    Change in index of labor cost per unit of output, manufacturing, smoothed
    Average prime rate charged by banks
    Commercial and industrial loans outstanding in 1982 dollars
    Ratio, consumer installment credit outstanding to personal income
    Change in consumer price index for services, smoothed

Source: U.S. Department of Commerce, Bureau of Economic Analysis, *Survey of*

Current Business, 73 (October 1993), 12-15.

Reading the Index of Leading Indicators

Of the three composite indexes, the one that attracts the most attention each month is the composite index of 11 leading indicators, which is often abbreviated as the index of leading indicators. The trend of the Composite Index of 11 Leading Indicators in recent years is reprinted on the next page from the March 1994 issue of the *Survey of Current Business*, published by the U.S. Department of Commerce.

The peak and trough months of recessions are indicated vertically in the figure. The numbers shown above the leading indicators curve are the lead time in months between the beginning of the decline in the index and the beginning of the recession. The numbers shown below the index curve, on the other hand, are the lead time in months between the beginning of the increase in the index and the end of the recession.

The index of leading indicators does lead turning points of economic fluctuations. The lead time, however, varies widely. The lead months for recessions range from three months for the 1980 recession to as long as 23 months for the 1957-58 recession. In other words, the 1980 recession began only three months after the index of leading indicators started declining, whereas the 1957-58 recession began almost two years after the index started declining.

The lead time for recovery is considerably shorter and ranges from one to eight months. The number in the box located at the upper right-hand corner is the latest month of which the data are included in the graph.

The index of leading indicators does show the overall strength of the economy. Some have suggested a rule of thumb: If the index falls for three consecutive months, the fall indicates that a recession is coming. The relation between fluctuations in the index and fluctuations in real GDP, however, is too loose to forecast turning points of the economy using the index. It is not unusual for no recession to occur even after the index falls for several consecutive months.

CYCLICAL INDICATORS

Composite Indexes

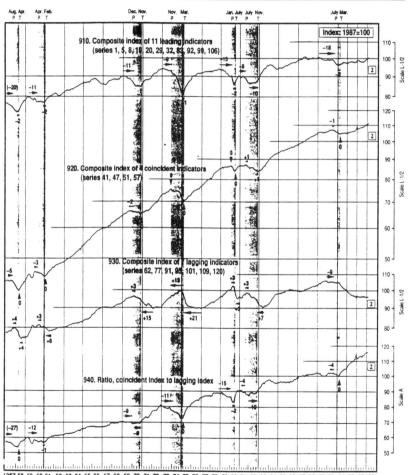

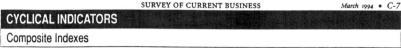

910. Composite index of 11 leading indicators
(series 1, 5, 8, 19, 20, 29, 32, 83, 92, 99, 106)

Index: 1987=100

920. Composite index of 4 coincident indicators
(series 41, 47, 51, 57)

930. Composite index of 7 lagging indicators
(series 62, 77, 91, 95, 101, 109, 120)

940. Ratio, coincident index to lagging index

1957 58 59 60 61 62 63 64 65 66 67 68 69 70 71 72 73 74 75 76 77 78 79 80 81 82 83 84 85 06 87 88 89 90 91 92 93 1994

NOTE — The numbers and arrows indicate length of leads (-) and lags (+) in months from business
cycle turning dates. Current data for these series are shown on page C-1.

According to Anderson and Erceg, if the composite index of leading indicators has declined in four of the last seven months, the chances are two out of three that a business peak will occur sometime within the next 14 months. Also, if the composite index of leading indicators has risen for two consecutive months, the chances are three to one that a trough will be reached in the next one to nine months.[2]

Business Forecasting

Perhaps, the most important forecasting that businesses have to do is sales forecasting. Sales are simply consumer demand viewed from businesses. Sales forecasting model is a demand function for the company's product. A sales forecasting model, therefore, needs to include the following basic variables:

$$S = f(P, P_r, Y, C, O) \qquad (13\text{-}11)$$

where S = sales
P = price of the product
P_r = prices of substitutes and complements
Y = income or purchasing power
C = number of consumers
O = other variables unique to the product.

Variations: Seasonal Adjustment

As we studied in Chapter 5, any sales forecasting model based on seasonal fluctuations needs to incorporate seasonal fluctuations in the model if sales fluctuate from one month to the next or from one season to the next. If sales fluctuate from one quarter to the next, for instance, equation (13-11) changes to:

$$S = f(P, P_r, Y, C, O, \Sigma Q_i) \qquad (13\text{-}14)$$

where $i = 1, 2,$ and 3.
If sales fluctuate from one month to the next, equation (13-14) changes

to:

$$S = f(P, P_r, Y, C, O, \Sigma Q_i) \qquad (13\text{-}15)$$

where $i = 1, 2, ..., 11$.

Notice that there are only 11 dummy variables for 12 months. This is because we drop one dummy in order to avoid matrix singularity. The one dummy dropped can be any of the 12 months. A general practice is to drop any of monthly dummy variables, the estimated coefficients of which are statistically insignificant.

Variations: Expectations

Alternatively, forecasters may utilize an expectations approach. A simplest expectations approach would be static expectation in which the next year's sales forecasts (S^f_{+1}) would be same as this year's actual sales (S):

$$S^f_{+1} = S \qquad (13\text{-}16)$$

Another simple rule would be adaptive expectations. In this view, forecasters update their expectations about future depending on the extent to which their expectations about the present period turned out to be wrong. According to adaptive expectations, the next year's sales forecasts (S^f_{+1}) are obtained by updating this year's sales forecasts made last year (S^f) by a fraction γ (read as gamma) of the forecast error. That is,

$$S^f_{+1} = S^f + \gamma(S - S^f) \qquad (13\text{-}17)$$

Rearranging,

$$\begin{aligned} S^f_{+1} &= S^f + \gamma S - \gamma S^f & (13\text{-}18) \\ &= (1 - \gamma)S^f + \gamma S & (13\text{-}19) \end{aligned}$$

If $\gamma = 0$ so that expectations remain unchanged from one year to the next, $S^f_{+1} = S^f$, prompting the poem:[3]

How to Forecast Revenue

To find a value good and true,
Here are three things for you to do:
Consider your replacement cost,
Determine value that is lost,
Analyze your sales to see
What market value really should be
Now if these suggestions are not clear,
Copy the figures you used last year.

Summary

Businesses need to know what lies ahead in the national and regional economy so that they can prepare a fast growth by accelerating the production process and prepare a slowdown by reducing their production and tightening inventories. National forecasts are usually made by econometric methods based on either the classical economics or Keynesian economics.

Classical economics is characterized by *laissez faire* philosophy, flexible prices and wages, full employment equilibrium, and the quantity theory of money. When the Great Depression started in 1929 and showed no sign of ending as prescribed by the classical economics, Keynesian economics emerged. Keynesian economics is characterized by inflexible prices and wages at least downwardly and a greater role of government in the economy through fiscal policy.

In econometric forecasting, the values of exogenous variables are assumed to be given to the model *a priori* and the values of endogenous variables are determined within the model. Econometric models allow a sensitivity analysis which tests how sensitive the value of the dependent variable is to changes in the value of exogenous variables.

Economists track business cycles through the use of cyclical indicators. Among the three types of indicators of leading, coincident, and lagging indicators, the composite index of 11 leading indicators is most widely watched. Although the index of leading indicators does show the overall strength of the economy, the lead time between changes in the index and changes in the economy is not consistent. According to Anderson and Erceg, if the composite index of leading indicators has declined in four of the last seven months, the chances are two out of three that a business peak will occur sometime within the next 14 months. Also, if the composite index of leading indicators has risen for two consecutive months, the chances are three to one that a trough will be reached in the next one to nine months.

Sales forecasting model is equivalent to a demand function, and needs to include key variables that a demand function contains. These include price, income, advertising, and prices of complements and substitutes. Seasonal forecasting models may utilize dummy variables that represent seasonal changes.

Endnotes

1. There is no consensus regarding the end of the classical school. Many economists prefer to cite 1871 as the end of the classical school. That was the year when William Stanley Jevons (1835-1882) and Carl Menger (1840-1921) published their works on marginal revenue, marginal cost, and other concepts known as marginalism.

2. Gerald H. Anderson and John J. Erceg, "Forecasting Turning Points with Leading Indicators," Federal Reserve Bank of Cleveland *Economic Commentary*, October 1, 1989, pp. 1-4.

3. Source: Anonymous, quoted from *Poverty taxation: Effects on Land Uses and Local Government Revenues*, A study prepared for the Subcommittee on Intergovernmental Relations of the Senate Committee on Government Operations, 92nd Congress,

1st Session, 1971, p. 29.

Chapter 14

Pricing and Profit Analysis

If we ask firms what their pricing objectives are, we are likely to hear many different answers.[1] These may include achieving a target rate of return on investment, maintaining or expanding a market share, stabilizing prices, and meeting competitors. No matter how these objectives may be stated, the bottom line in pricing objectives is to maximize the present value of future profit streams. In this chapter, we study topics that may assist business managers in pursuing the pricing policy that brings them a maximum profit.

Profit Contribution

A favorite behavioral assumption that economists make when studying production activities of firms is that firms optimize the use of resources by trying to maximize, not simply make, profits. Profit is the difference between total revenue and total cost. Total cost refers to total economic costs, which include implicit as well as explicit costs.

MR = MC Rule Revisited

Profits are maximized by producing a level of output at which the difference between total revenue and total cost is the greatest. The profit-maximizing level of output can also be determined by equating marginal revenue and marginal cost, as we studied in Chapter 9. The

MR = MC rule for profit maximization was obtained by taking the first derivative of the profit function:

$$\pi = TR(Q) - TC(Q) \qquad (9\text{-}4)$$
$$d\pi/dQ = TR'(Q) - TC'(Q)$$
$$= MR - MC = 0 \qquad (9\text{-}5)$$

Marginal revenue is the revenue from production and sale of the last unit of output, while marginal cost is the cost of producing the last unit of output. The **MR = MC rule** states that profits are maximized when firms produce the level of output at which marginal revenue is equal to marginal cost.

Marginal revenue and marginal cost are concepts used almost exclusively by economists. Business managers typically use the term profit contribution to describe what is essentially the difference between marginal revenue and marginal cost.

Defining Profit Contribution

The **profit contribution** of a product is the difference between revenue from sales of the product and the variable cost of its production. The profit contribution is usually expressed on the per unit basis:

$$PC = P - AVC \qquad (14\text{-}1)$$

where PC = profit contribution
  P = price of product
  AVC = average variable cost of production

In the marginal analysis, the profit for the last unit of output (PLU) is the difference between marginal revenue (MR) and marginal cost (MC):

$$PLU = MR - MC \qquad (14\text{-}2)$$

The question is: Under what conditions will the profit contribution (PC) in equation (14-1) be equal to the profit for the last unit (PLU) in equation (14-2)?

Consider firms in reality. Most firms do not change prices every day or even every week. So long as the price of a product remains constant, as it usually does for any reasonable range of sales, price (P) is equal to marginal revenue (MR). The average variable cost is also not likely to change as output changes within a reasonable range. If the average variable cost remains unchanged, the average variable cost (AVC) is equal to marginal cost (MC). The concept of profit contribution, therefore, is a good approximation of the difference between marginal revenue and marginal cost. Because of its simplicity, it is profit contribution, not marginal revenue nor marginal cost, that is used by managers of firms in making pricing decisions.

Illustrations

Consider the Emperor Clock Company in Fairhope, Alabama, which specializes in making grandfather clocks. Suppose that the retail price of a typical grandfather clock is $800, the average variable cost of making the clock is $500, and the clock's share of fixed costs is $200, leaving the remaining $100 to net profits.

Suppose that a traveler from Texas to Florida stops by the store and offers a final price of $600. If all grandfather clocks were sold below the full cost of $700, the firm would go out of business. For business at the margin such as the traveler's offer of $600, however, the firm's profit would increase if the clock were sold at $600 to the traveler. The profit contribution from the sale would be $100 since the sale price is $600 and the average variable cost is $500. The profit contribution would be used toward paying the fixed cost. Remember that the traveler is not expected to tell the store's regular customers how much he or she paid for the clock and thus adversely affect the store's regular sales.

For another application of the concept of the profit contribution, consider Electronics Company that sells pocket calendar at a selling price of $21 per unit. The company's cost per unit based on the full capacity of 200,000 units is as follows:

Direct materials	$ 4
Direct labor	5
Shipping costs	3
Overhead (two-thirds of which is fixed)	6

Total	$18

Suppose that a special order offering to buy 20,000 units was received from a foreign distributor. The company has sufficient existing capacity to manufacture the additional units. In negotiating a price for the special order, Electronics should consider that the minimum selling price per unit should be $14, obtained as the sum of direct materials ($4), direct labor ($5), shipping costs ($3), and the portion of fixed cost that is allocated, rather than truly fixed. The allocated fixed cost is one-third of $6, which is $2.

Pricing Practices of Firms

Although the long-term objective in pricing is to maximize the present value of future profit streams, short-term pricing objectives can vary. For example, managers of firms may consider: **loss leader pricing** in which a firm prices a product below its cost in order to attract customers; **predatory pricing** in which a firm cuts price in order to drive competitors out of the market; and **limit pricing** in which a firm prices a new product below the minimum average cost of production in order to prevent new entries into the market for the product. One economic concept that plays the role of a motherlode for all different pricing objectives is the price elasticity of demand.

Price Elasticity in Pricing

Ideally, businesses would be happy to charge a price that covers full cost of production and a desired mark-up. The markup depends on the extent of competition that the firm is facing. The more competition there is, the more substitutes there are and the more elastic the demand for the product is. When the demand is price-elastic, the price will have to be lowered to increase total revenue. Other things being equal, there is an inverse relation between price and the price elasticity of demand for the product.

One interesting application of this inverse relation between price and the price elasticity of demand is the pricing strategy when the payment is made by a third party.

When payments for service are made by a party that does not directly benefit from the service, the price elasticity of demand for the service tends to be relatively inelastic. One example would be fees for medical services that are paid by insurance companies. In this case, patients become less sensitive to fees and change behavior in such a way to maximize medical services with no constraint to prices. This increases demand for services and the increased demand makes the service less price-elastic at the existing price. Providers of medical services then can raise price to increase total revenue.

The tendency for higher prices when payments are made by a third party also applies to Medicare (for the elderly) and Medicaid (for the poor), as well as any contractual services made with the public sector. For the same service, for instance, attorneys and business consultants are likely to charge higher fees to the public sector.

The impact of a third-party payment on the price of a product may also explain why textbooks are expensive. Textbooks are selected by professors who do not pay. The professors' demand for textbooks, therefore, is quite inelastic, enabling publishers of textbooks to raise their prices. A limited price competition in textbook markets has been encouraged through the co-ops of student organizations or the formation of bookstores near the campus that are unaffiliated with the university bookstore. A further competition may be possible through a conscientious adoption of textbooks by professors who may provide optional textbooks of similar quality to students.

Odd Pricing

Professor Lee Kreul of Purdue University's School of Consumer and

Family Sciences reviewed 467 prices in advertisements placed by 242 restaurants in 24 newspapers.[2] When a restaurant placed advertisements for meals that cost less than $7, the price usually ended with the number 9, such as the prices $3.99 or $4.99, but when a restaurant placed advertisements for meals costing $7 to $10, the price usually ended with the number 5, such as the prices $7.95 or $8.95. Kreul suggests that the pricing practices of restaurants are intended to provide a discount illusion. Restaurants change the ending number of a price from 9 to 5 as the price of meals increases beyond $7 because more than one cent is required to create the discount illusion for these higher priced meals, but patrons interested in meals costing more than $7 might perceive a price ending in the number 9 as indicating low quality or sloppy service.

Quoted prices in department stores, catalogs, and televised advertising frequently are of the form $2.99, $399, and $1,098. The practice of ending a price in 9 or 8 cannot be explained by marginal cost pricing since the probability that most marginal costs end just one cent or one dollar below a round number is very small. Professors Gabrielle Brenner and Reuven Brenner suggest the hypothesis that the practice is based on the limited capacity of our brains for storing directly accessible information.[3] When a price is $398, for instance, the consumer tries to remember first that the price is $300, or perhaps that it is $390, but rarely does he or she remember that it is exactly $398. Why do consumers not round the number from, say, $398 to $400 and then store it? According to Brenner and Brenner, immediately after the message, consumers are exposed to additional information such as another advertisement. The information on price, therefore, must be stored very quickly, and the quickest way to do so is by storing the first digits.

Another hypothesis on why stores charge odd prices, such as $.99, $1.99, $29.99, etc. was suggested by a 10-year-old reader of Dean Ann Landers.[4] According to the reader, around 1875, Melville Stone owned a newspaper named the Chicago Daily News. The price was a penny. Circulation was good, but after a while it began to drop off. He found that it was because pennies were in short supply. Mr. Stone persuaded Chicago merchants to sell their merchandise for a penny below the regular price. This put more pennies in circulation and it helped save the paper. The reader identified the source of the story as *Why didn't I think of that?* by Webb Garison.

Pricing Guidelines

Business managers may also consider pricing guidelines suggested by Grant, Smith and ...:[5]

You're gouging on your prices if you
Charge more than the rest.
But it's unfair competition
If you think you can charge less.
A second point that we would make
To help avoid confusion:
Don't try to charge the same amount.
That would be collusion!
You must compete. But not too much,
For if you do, you see,
Then the market would be yours
And that's monopoly!

Breakeven Analysis

One important question that all business managers want to have an answer of is: How much do we have to sell to break even? The answer is provided in a breakeven analysis. To break even,

$$TR = TC \qquad\qquad (14\text{-}3)$$

Since $TR = P \times Q$, $TC = FC + VC$, and $VC = AVC \times Q$, we rewrite (14-3):

$$P \times Q = FC + AVC \times Q \qquad (14\text{-}4)$$

Solving for Q

$$P \times Q - AVC \times Q = FC$$
$$(P - AVC)Q = FC$$
$$Q = FC/(P - AVC) \qquad (14\text{-}5)$$

The numerator in (14-5) is a firm's total fixed cost, and the denominator is the profit contribution per unit of the product. The value of Q, when computed in (14-5), is the quantity that is needed for the firm to break even.

The same expression can easily be extended to determine the sales volume necessary to achieve a profit objective. Assuming that the profit objective is PO. Expression (14-3) changes to

$$TR = TC + PO \qquad (14\text{-}6)$$

Solving (14-6) for Q as we did in (14-4), we obtain

$$Q = (FC + PO)/(P - AVC). \qquad (14\text{-}7)$$

For illustration of a breakeven analysis, let us suppose that a manufacturer sells his product at \$5 per unit; the fixed cost is \$3,000; and the variable cost is 40 percent of total revenue. The breakeven quantity of sales can be found;

$$TR = 5Q \qquad (14\text{-}8)$$
$$TC = 3,000 + .4(TR) \qquad (14\text{-}9)$$
$$= 3,000 + 2Q$$
$$TR = TC \qquad (14\text{-}10)$$
$$5Q = 3,000 + 2Q$$
$$Q = 1,000 \text{ units.} \qquad (14\text{-}11)$$

Key Business Ratios

There are a number of business ratios that businesses frequently compile. These ratios may be used for further improvement of managerial efficiency, acquisition of other firms, reporting to the board of directors and regulatory agencies, and the like. Key ratios are defined in this section on the basis of Industry Norms by Dun & Bradstreet Credit Services and numerous other sources.

Solvency

Current Liabilities to Inventory. This ratio indicates the extent to which the business relies on funds from disposal of unsold inventories to meet its debts. This ratio, combined with Net Sales to Inventory, indicates how management controls inventory.

Current Liabilities to Net Worth. This ratio contrasts the funds that creditors temporarily are risking with the funds permanently invested by the owners. The smaller the net worth and the larger the liabilities, the less security for the creditors. Care should be exercised when selling any firm with current liabilities exceeding two-thirds (66.6 percent) of net worth.

Current Ratio. Total current assets are divided by total current liabilities. Current assets include cash, accounts and notes receivable (less reserves for bad debts), advances on inventories, merchandise inventories, and marketable securities. This ratio measures the ability of a firm to meet its current obligations. Other things being equal, the higher the current ratio, the more assurance the creditors have about being paid in full and on time. The current ratio measures the margin of safety available to cover any possible shrinkage in the value of current assets. Normally a ratio of 2 to 1 (2.0) or better is considered good.

Debt Service Coverage. Debt service is the outlay needed, supplied or accrued for such payments during any accounting period.

Fixed Assets to Net Worth. The proportion of net worth that consists of fixed assets will vary greatly from industry to industry but generally a smaller proportion is desirable. A high ratio is unfavorable because heavy investment in fixed assets indicates that either the concern has a low net working capital and is overtrading or has utilized large funded debt to supplement working capital. Also, the larger the fixed assets, the bigger the annual depreciation charge that must be deducted from the income statement. Normally, fixed assets above 75 percent of net worth indicate possible over-investment and should be examined with care.

Quick Ratio. Computed by dividing cash plus accounts receivable by total current liabilities. Current liabilities are all the liabilities that fall due within one year. This ratio reveals the protection afforded short-term creditors in cash or near-cash assets. It shows the number of dollars of liquid assets available to cover each dollar of current debt. Any time this ratio is as much as 1 to 1 (1.0) the business is said to be in a liquid condition. The larger the ratio the greater the liquidity.

Total Liabilities to Net Worth. Obtained by dividing total current plus long-term and deferred liabilities by net worth. The effect of long-term (funded) debt on a business can be determined by comparing this ratio with Current Liabilities to Net Worth. The difference will pinpoint the relative size of long-term debt, which, if sizable, can burden a firm with substantial interest charges. In general total liabilities shouldn't exceed net worth (100 percent) since in such cases creditors have more at stake than owners.

Efficiency

Accounts Payable to Sales. This ratio measures how the company is paying its suppliers in relation to the volume being transacted. An increasing percentage, or one larger than the industry norm, indicates the firm may be using suppliers to help finance operations. This ratio is especially important to short-term creditors since a high percentage could indicate potential problems in paying vendors.

Assets to Sales. Calculated by dividing total assets by annual net sales. This ratio ties in sales and the total investment that is used to generate those sales. While figures vary greatly from industry to industry, by comparing a company's ratio with industry norms it can be determined whether a firm is overtrading (handling an excessive volume of sales in relation to investment) or undertrading (not generating sufficient sales to warrant the assets invested). Abnormally low percentages (below the lower quartile) can indicate overtrading which may lead to financial difficulties if not corrected. Extremely high percentages (above the upper quartile) can be the result of overly conservative or poor sales management, indicating a more aggressive sales policy may need to be followed.

Collection Period. Accounts receivable are divided by sales and then multiplied by 365 days to obtain this figure. The quality of the receivables of a company can be determined by this relationship when compared with selling terms and industry norms. In some industries where credit sales are not the normal way of doing business, the percentage of cash sales should be taken into consideration. Generally, where most sales are for credit, any collection period more than one-third over normal selling terms (40.0 for 30-day terms) is indicative of some slow-turning receivables. When comparing the collection period of one concern with that of another, allowances should be made for possible variations in selling terms.

Days in Accounts Receivable. Shows the average time required to collect receivables.

Debt to Equity. Measures the amount of leverage used by a company. Investors generally prefer a higher debt to equity ratio while creditors favor a lower ratio. Higher debt to equity ratios reflect greater stability and lower risk concerning the company's ability to pay its debt on time.

Net Sales to Inventory. Obtained by dividing annual net sales by inventory. Inventory control is a prime management objective since poor controls allow inventory to become costly to store, obsolete or insufficient to meet demands. The sales-to-inventory relationship is a guide to the rapidity at which merchandise is being moved and the effect on the flow of funds into the business. This ratio varies widely between different lines of business and a company's figure is only meaningful when compared with industry norms. Individual figures that are outside either the upper or lower quartiles for a given industry should be examined with care. Although low figures are usually the biggest problem, as they indicate excessively high inventories, extremely high turnovers might reflect insufficient merchandise to meet customer demand and result in lost sales.

Operating Margin. Measures a firm's effectiveness in generating earnings for a give sales volume. This ratio varies widely from one industry to another, so comparisons with industry ratios are generally the pertinent ones.

Sales to Net Working Capital. Net sales are divided by net working capital. Net working capital is current assets minus current liabilities. This relationship indicates whether a company is overtrading or conversely carrying more liquid assets than needed for its volume. Each industry can vary substantially and it is necessary to compare a company with its peers to see if it is either overtrading on its available funds or being overly conservative. Companies with substantial sales gains often reach a level where their working capital becomes strained. Even if they maintain an adequate total investment for the volume being generated (Assets to Sales), that investment may be so centered in fixed assets or other non-current items that it will be difficult to continue meeting all current obligations without additional investment or reducing sales.

Profitability

Return on Assets. Net profit after taxes divided by total assets. This ratio is the key indicator of profitability for a firm. It matches operating profits with the assets available to earn a return. Companies efficiently using their assets will have a relatively high return while less well-run businesses will be relatively low. Same as return on assets in service except in this case only assets at the beginning of the year or either only assets at the end of the year were used to calculate the ratio. Return on assets in service uses the average between the two.

Return on Net Worth (Return on Equity). Obtained by dividing net profit after tax by net worth. This ratio is used to analyze the ability of the firm's management to realize an adequate return on the capital invested by the owners of the firm. **Return on Equity.** This ratio measures the rate of return on average fund balance for the hospital. Tendency is to look increasingly to this ratio as a final criterion of profitability. Generally, a relationship of at least 10 percent is regarded as a desirable objective for providing dividends plus funds for future growth.

Return on Sales (Profit Margin). Obtained by dividing net profit after taxes by annual net sales. This reveals the profits earned per dollar of sales and therefore measures the efficiency of the operation. Return must be adequate for the firm to be able to achieve satisfactory profits for its owners. This ratio is an indicator of the firm's ability to withstand adverse conditions such as falling prices, rising costs and declining sales.

Summary

The profit contribution of a product is the difference between revenue from sales of the product and the variable cost of its production. The profit contribution is equal to the difference between marginal revenue and marginal cost so long as price and average cost remain stable.

Firms price products to maximize the present value of future profit streams. Short-term pricing objectives vary. In loss leader pricing, a firm prices a product below its cost in order to attract customers; in predatory pricing, a firm cuts price in order to drive competitors out of the market; and in limit pricing, a firm prices a new product below the minimum average cost of production in order to prevent new entries into the market for the product. The markup of a product price varies inversely with the price elasticity of demand. The practice of ending a retail price with "9" is explained in several different ways, which include consumers' difficulty to store information quickly, and the past shortage of pennies.

When payments are made by a third party who does not directly benefits, or when a choice is made by a party that does not pay, the demand for the good or service becomes less price-elastic and their prices tend to go up. Examples are medical services that are paid by the government or insurance companies and the selection of textbooks made by professors but paid by students.

The breakeven quantity of sales is obtained by dividing fixed cost by the profit contribution, while the profit requirement is obtained by dividing the sum of fixed cost and required profit by the profit contribution.

Key business ratios are compiled by businesses for many purposes including improvement of managerial efficiency, acquisition of other firms, and reporting to the board of directors and regulatory agencies. These ratios are grouped into solvency ratios, efficiency ratios, and profitability ratios.

Endnotes

1.   R. F. Lanzillotti, "Pricing Objectives in Large Companies," *American Economic Review*, 48 (December 1958), 924-927.
2.   Jack C. Horn, "The High-Class Nickel Discount," *Psychology Today*, September 1982, p. 18.
3.   Gabrielle A. Brenner and Reuven Brenner, "Memory and Markets, or Why Are You Paying $2.99 for a Widget?" *The Journal of Business*, 55 (January 1982) 147-158.
4.   *Mobile Register*, August 4, 1987, p. 7-B.
5.   R.W. Grant, "Tom Smith and His Incredible Bread Machine," quoted from Earl L. Bailey (ed.), *Pricing Practices and Strategies*, (New York: The Conference Board, 1978), p. 18.

Chapter 15

Capital Budgeting and Feasibility Studies

Capital budgeting is the process of evaluating a profitability of major investment projects. These projects may be private sector projects such as building a major manufacturing plant or purchasing a new machine that may significantly lower long-run costs of production. Private sector projects may also include development of an upscale subdivision with a golf course or a shopping center. Examples of public sector projects that require capital budgeting may include new highway projects, new convention centers or government office complexes, and major military procurement projects such as building a new aircraft carrier.

An Overview

Two important steps in the capital budgeting process are estimating cash flows generated by a particular investment and determining the rate of return required on the investment. After cash flows have been estimated and the cost of capital has been determined, the next step is an evaluation of the worth of an investment project. According to surveys of current practice among large U.S. firms, the most common technique used by these firms is the net present value approach, the internal rate of return approach, or both.[1]

Net Present Value

The **net present value** (NPV) of an investment is simply the present value of the cash flows minus the capital outlay. The net present value of an investment is defined as

$$NPV = \sum_{i=1}^{n} \frac{R_i}{(1 + k)^i} - I_o \qquad (15\text{-}1)$$

where R_i is the expected cash flow generated by a particular capital project in year "i", and "k" is the required rate of return on the cash flow. The net present value of a capital project is determined (a) by projecting future cash flows from the investment; (b) by converting the expected future cash flows to their present values; (c) by adding up the present values of all expected cash flows from year 1 through year "n", where "n" is the year of the last expected cash flow generated by the project; and (d) by subtracting from the sum of present values the initial capital outlay that is invested. The term "k" is the rate of return required to "penalize" cash flows for both time and risk. According to the net present value approach, projects with higher net present values are preferred to those with lower net present values.

Internal Rate of Return

The net present value measures the dollar value of a profitability of any capital project. In comparison, the internal rate of return measures the rate of return expected to be earned on an investment if the expected cash flows materialize. The **internal rate of return** is defined as the rate of return that, when used as the discount rate, discounts the future cash flows so that their present value is equal to the initial cash outlay on the investment.

The internal rate of return is a rearrangement of the net present value

$$\sum_{i=1}^{n} \frac{R_i}{(1 + k)^i} = I_o \qquad (15\text{-}2)$$

where k is the internal rate of return. Note that the internal rate of return stated in (15-2) is simply the net present value set equal to zero:

$$NPV = \sum_{i=1}^{n} \frac{R_i}{(1 + k)^i} - I_o = 0 \qquad (15\text{-}3)$$

Benefit-Cost Ratio

The benefit-cost ratio is another way of measuring benefits from a project to its cost. The benefit-cost ratio is based on the same data used to estimate the project's net present value. To be specific, the **benefit-cost ratio** is another rearrangement of the net present value expression, which is:

$$\frac{\sum_{i=1}^{n} \frac{R_i}{(1 + k)^i}}{I_o} \qquad (15\text{-}4)$$

In other words, the cost of investment is divided into the sum of present values rather than subtracted from it as was the case in the net present value approach. According to the benefit-cost ratio approach, projects with higher B/C ratios are preferred to those with lower B/C ratios.

Payback Period

The **payback period** method refers to calculating the time period that is necessary for an investment to generate a cash flow equal in amount to the initial outlay required for the investment. The payback period method is a simple technique used widely to determine the minimum time period that is needed to generate a cash flow beyond the initial investment.

Multicriteria Evaluation

A recent approach toward evaluation of major public sector projects is to look beyond economic criteria such as benefit-cost ratios or net present values. Factors beyond economic criteria include opinions of public officials, impact of the project as perceived by the area's residents, the impact of the proposed project on the area's land use, and the like. Evaluation process of the multicriteria evaluation, therefore, tends to take into consideration multiple socio-economic and environmental consequences. Considering the need to account for these diverse influences of public sector projects, some have suggested that an appropriate approach toward evaluating major public sector projects would be the multicriteria evaluation approach.[2]

Numerical Illustration

Presented in this section is a simple example of a capital budgeting problem that can be calculated using a pen and paper, or at the most a small calculator. This example is designed to show the difference among the net present value, the internal rate of return, and the payback period approaches.

Suppose that a firm is considering a capital investment project. The project requires an initial investment of $70,000 and is expected to generate annual cash flows of $40,000 for the first year, $50,000 for the second year, and $50,000 for the third and final year. Due to the riskiness of the project, the required rate of return is 20 percent. We would like to determine the net present value, the internal rate of return, and the payback period of the project.

The net present value (NPV) of the project is obtained:

$$NPV = 40,000/(1 + 0.2) + 50,000/(1 + 0.2)^2$$
$$+ 50,000/(1 + 0.2)^3 - 70,000 \qquad (15\text{-}5)$$
$$= 33,333 + 34,722 + 28,935 - 70,000$$
$$= 26,990 \qquad\qquad\qquad (15\text{-}6)$$

The internal rate of return (r) is found by a trial and error method. According to the internal rate of return approach,

$$40,000/(1 + r) + 50,000/(1 + r)^2 + 50,000/(1 + r)^3 = 70,000 \quad (15\text{-}7)$$

At $r = .40$, the left-side of (15-7) is 72,303; at $r = 0.45$, the left-side amount is 67,768. A further trial indicates that at $r = 0.4247$, the left-side of (15-7) is most close to 70,000. The internal rate of return is 42.47 percent.

Finally, the payback period is obtained as follows. The first year cash flow is 40,000. We thus subtract 40,000 from 70,000. To determine the days during the second year that are needed to generate the total cash flow of 70,000, we estimate

$$365 \times (70,000 - 40,000)/50,000 = 219 \quad (15\text{-}8)$$

The payback period is 1 year and 219 days.

Feasibility Studies

The role of business managers in capital budgeting is two-fold; undertaking feasibility studies and carrying out the projects. Carrying out the projects to their completion is a managerial task beyond the scope of managerial economics. Feasibility studies are clearly within the realm of managerial economics. Business managers may undertake feasibility studies for themselves or more likely through employment of economists or economic consulting firms. Presented in this chapter are the outlines of a highway project as an example of public sector projects and the development of a subdivision as an example of private sector projects.

Feasibility of a Highway Project

Perhaps, the most popular approach toward evaluation of a highway project is the benefit-cost analysis. Economic benefits of a new highway have two components; transportation benefits and economic development benefits.

Transportation benefits include the dollar value of savings in travel time for passenger vehicles as well as trucks, savings in operation and maintenance costs of vehicles, the dollar value of reduced fatality, and the dollar value of reduced non-fatal accidents.

Development benefits include short-term benefits from expenditures of construction dollars and long-term economic development benefits. The short-term impact from expenditures of construction dollars is an opportunity cost, which may be of interest to the corridor residents but not to the government. The government can easily spend these construction dollars on other projects outside the corridor area for the same expenditure impact. The short-term benefits, therefore, should not be included in estimating the benefits from the new highway.

The long-term development benefits arise, first, from economic development based on the new highway as an added infrastructure that may attract new industries to the corridor area and, second, from rising visitor activities and roadside businesses such as motels and gas stations. Put differently, the corridor area is expected to benefit from long-term changes in land-use patterns that the new highway is likely to generate.

Economic costs of building the highway are the sum of labor and material costs of constructing the highway, right-of-way costs, periodic resurfacing costs, and reduced property tax revenue from right-of-way acquisitions.

To summarize the economic methodology,

$$B = B_T + B_E \qquad\qquad (15\text{-}9)$$
$$B_T = T_V + T_M + T_F + T_N \quad (15\text{-}10)$$
$$B_E = D_W + D_V \qquad\qquad (15\text{-}11)$$
$$C = C_C + C_R + C_S + C_T \qquad (15\text{-}12)$$
$$B/C \text{ ratio} = B/C \qquad\qquad (15\text{-}13)$$

where
B = benefits from the connector
B_T = transportation benefits
T_V = dollar value of savings in travel time

T_M = savings in operation and maintenance costs of vehicles
T_F = dollar value of reduced fatality
T_N = dollar value of reduced non-fatal accidents
B_E = development benefits
D_W = development benefits through attraction of new industries
D_V = development benefits from rising visitor activities and roadside businesses
C = costs of building the connector
C_C = labor and material costs of constructing the highway
C_R = right-of-way costs
C_S = resurfacing costs, and
C_T = reduced property tax revenue.

All benefits and costs are estimated for a 30-year project life, but are converted to constant dollars for the reference year during which the decision is made for or against the construction.

Selective Issues on the Model

Although the final outcome of an economic evaluation is presented in definitive benefit-cost ratios, the process of deriving these ratios is not as straightforward as may appear in the model summarized as equations (15-5) through (15-9). The process requires a value judgment on several issues. Three such issues are reviewed in this section; economic development benefits, multiplier effect, and the selection of a discount rate.

Economic Development Benefits

There is a controversy, especially concerning federal highway projects, as to whether economic development benefits should be included in estimation of benefits from the project. The economic development benefits have two components; short-term benefits from direct expenditures of the construction dollars, and long-term benefits that arise from the new highway as an added infrastructure.

It is easy to understand why short-term benefits should not be counted as benefits specific to the project, since construction dollars are clearly opportunity costs that can easily be spent elsewhere generating comparable expenditure benefits. What about long-term development benefits? If short-term construction benefits are opportunity costs, shouldn't long-term development benefits arising from expenditure of construction dollars also be opportunity costs? This is a tough question, since not many highway projects can be justified based solely on transportation benefits. Also, highway projects provide an infrastructure, the benefits of which spread widely over a large number of industries and can hardly be measured.

Strictly speaking, long-term development benefits may also be considered an opportunity cost, since these benefits arise ultimately from the same expenditures that generate the short-term economic impact. According to this view, long-term development benefits should be included only if they exceed the average long-term development benefits when the same dollars are spent on all public sector projects including highway projects. There are no direct references that estimate the average long-term development benefits of public sector projects.

If development benefits are included in estimation of benefits, it is necessary to forecast population in the study area with or without the new highway. The model of forecasting the impact of the new highway on counties may be described as

$$Y_t = Y_o e^{(r + \Delta r)t} \qquad (15\text{-}14)$$

where Y_o = population/employment in base year
  t = year; $t = 0$ in year 2000
  Y_t = population/employment in year t
  r = annual rate of growth without the new connector
  Δr = increase in the growth rate with the connector

Equation (15-14) without Δr is equivalent to the equation for baseline forecasts. There are two ways of estimating the value of Δr; econometric and judgmental. If the project involves an area that is not conducive to developing an econometric model, a judgmental approach would be necessary. Judgmental approach requires review of many previous studies.[3]

Multiplier Effect

Expenditures on major highway projects tend to generate secondary expenditures impact, known as the multiplier effect. The multiplier effect is usually not included in estimating benefits. There are two reasons for this practice. First, the normal size of multiplier 2 requires a fairly large-size population and economic base. When the proposed highway passes through many small cities and towns, the size of the multiplier is likely to be quite small, if any. More importantly, the first round construction expenditures are not included in estimating the benefits, since these dollars represent opportunity costs. The short-term multiplier effect cannot be added when the first round expenditures that generate the multiplier effect are not included.

Selection of a Discount Rate

In computing the benefit-cost ratio, future benefits and costs need to be converted to present values. The conversion requires the selection of a discount rate. Since the discount rate selected is frequently a real discount rate rather than a nominal discount rate, it is important to understand the difference between a nominal interest rate and a real interest rate.

The rate of inflation (f) is the change in prices from the preceding period (P_{-1}) to the present period (P), divided by the prices of the preceding period:

$$f = (P - P_{-1})/P_{-1} \qquad (15\text{-}15)$$

Let us multiply both sides of (15-15) by P_{-1}, update the time period by

1, and rearrange:

$$f \times P_{-1} = P - P_{-1}$$
$$f_{+1} \times P = P_{+1} - P$$
$$P + f_{+1} \times P = P_{+1}$$
$$P(1 + f_{+1}) = P_{+1}$$
$$P/P_{+1} = 1/(1 + f_{+1}) \qquad (15\text{-}16)$$

The real rate of interest (r) is the ratio of $P(1 + i)$, i.e., dollars available in period $(t + 1)$, divided by P_{+1}, i.e., the price in period $(t + 1)$, from which one is subtracted to measure net changes. Symbol "i" in $P(1 + i)$ stands for the nominal rate of interest:

$$r = P(1 + i)/P_{+1} - 1 \qquad (15\text{-}17)$$

Rearranging,

$$1 + r = P(1 + i)/P_{+1}$$
$$= (1 + i)P/P_{+1}$$
$$= (1 + i)/(1 + f_{+1}) \text{ since } P/P_{+1} = 1/(1 + f_{+1}) \text{ in } (15\text{-}16)$$

Solving for "r",

$$(1 + r)(1 + f_{+1}) = 1 + i$$
$$1 + f_{+1} + r + rf_{+1} = 1 + i$$
$$r = i - f_{+1} - rf_{+1} \qquad (15\text{-}18)$$

Or

$$r = i - f_{+1} \qquad (15\text{-}19)$$

since rf_{+1} is very small.

In summary, the current real rate of interest (r) is the current nominal rate of interest (i) minus the *future* rate of inflation. Equation (15-18) may be used for computation of the real rate of interest, but equation (15-19) is used for approximation of the real interest rate.

The real rate of interest has averaged two to three percent since the turn of the century. Also, the U.S. Supreme Court ruled in a personal injury case, *Jones v. Laughlin*, that "a judgment should not be reversed because of the [real] discount rate if it is between 1 and 3 percent."[4] Paragraph 8.b.(1) of the **Office of Management and Budget Circular**

A-94, however, suggests that a 7 percent real discount rate be used in evaluation of highway projects. The use of 7 percent real discount rate tends to reduce the benefit-cost ratio, so long as the prevailing real interest rates remain below the 7 percent. This may cause the economic valuation of highway projects to be underestimated.

Feasibility of a Subdivision

A feasibility study of a large scale subdivision provides information on economic environment of the region, population and housing patterns in the immediate area, a neighborhood analysis describing in detail the surroundings of the property, and a market potential to indicate whether the project is likely to succeed or fail. Like any other land use project, the bottom line is to suggest the "best and highest valued use" of the land.

Market Potential

Perhaps, the most difficult part of a subdivision feasibility study is to figure out the market potential, or what is commonly known as the absorption rate. The estimation of market potential for the subdivision project requires consideration of several factors that will have a direct bearing on the housing market in the area. In a simplest form, the model of projecting the absorption rate of new housing units may be presented as follows.

Let POP stands for the area's population and Q^H stands for the number of owner-occupied housing units. By dividing the latter by the former, we obtain the ratio of owner-occupied housing units to the area's population:

$$Q^H_t \div POP_t = q_t \qquad (15\text{-}20)$$

and

$$Q^H_t = POP_t \times q_t \qquad (15\text{-}21)$$

in which "t" refers to the current period. In order to project the absorption rate, we need to project population for future years $(t+1)$ and make an assumption on the value of q in period $(t + 1)$. Since the ratio (q) is not expected to change rapidly, any short-term projections may assume that the value of q remains the same. The absorption rate, therefore, can be estimated by (15-22):

$$Q^H_{t+1} = POP_{t+1} \times q_{t+1} \qquad (15-22)$$

If the projection is made on the number of home sites (S^H_{t+1}) rather than homes, the value of Q^H_{t+1} may be increased by about 25 percent:

$$S^H_{t+1} = 1.25 \times Q^H_{t+1} \qquad (15-23)$$

The additional demand for home sites as opposed to homes comes from two sources. One relates to existing home owners living elsewhere who may buy lots with the intention to build homes or to resell the lots later. The other relates to builders who build "spec" (speculative) homes. For many new subdivisions, the demand for some sites is believed to be higher than the demand for homes by about 20 to 25 percent.

The procedure for estimating the market potential for an upscale subdivision, named Rock Creek, is illustrated in Table 15-1. We assume that the subdivision is being developed for homes that are at least $100,000 in price. The developer is interested in selling home sites, called lots, not in building homes.

As shown in Table 15-1, the area experienced a rapid population increase in the 1980s. The population increased by 33.2 percent. For projection purposes, the population is assumed to increase by another 35 percent from 1990 to 2000. The percent of owner-occupied homes in the area was 27.5 percent in 1980 and 29.3 percent in 1990. The percent is assumed to increase slowly to 31.2 percent. The number of owner-occupied housing units (15,288) in year 2000 is obtained by multiplying year 2000 population (49,000) by the 31.2 percent. Subtracting projected housing needs (15,288) in year 2000 from the actual housing units (10,632) in year 1990, we obtain the demand for new homes for the 1990s, which is 4,656 units.

Assume that we are interested in the number of homes priced $100,000 or more. The number of homes priced $100,000 plus in 1990 was 2,028 units, which constitutes 19.1 percent of all owner-occupied housing units. By assuming that this percentage increases to 20 percent, the number of homes priced $100,000 plus demanded in year 2000 is estimated as 3,058, which is obtained by multiplying the projected total owner-occupied homes (15,288) in year 2000 by 20 percent. Assuming that there is no inflation, the demand for new homes priced $100,000 plus during the 1990s is obtained by subtracting 2,028 from 3,058. The projected demand is 1,030. If we are interested in projecting home sites rather than new homes, the demand for home sites (1,288) is obtained by adding 25 percent to the demand for new homes (1,030). The annual absorption rate of new home sites in the area during the 1990s, therefore, is 129.

Table 15-1. Market Potential Analysis of Rock Creek

	1980	1990	2000
Area's population	27,241	36,296	49,000
percent change		33.2%	35.0%
Owner-occupied housing units	7,504	10,632	15,288
Percent of population	27.5%	29.3%	31.2%
Demand for new homes from 1990 to 2000			4,656
Homes $100,000+		2,028	3,058
Percent of all homes		19.1%	20.0%
Demand for new homes $100,000-plus			1,030
Demand for home sites for homes $100,000+			1,288
Annual increase in demand for home sites 19991 to 2000			129

Estimating the Present Value of Future Lost Earnings

Another interesting application of managerial economics is to estimate the present value of future lost earnings in personal injury cases.[5] The first step of the estimation procedure is to collect basic information relating to the case. Although the list may vary with the laws of the jurisdiction, the economist usually needs to find out for the injured or deceased person: (1) the name, (2) birth date, (3) sex, (4) race, (5) level of education, (6) date of accident, (7) nature of accident, (8) earnings record, (9) percent of fringe benefits if available, and (10) the judgment date for present value estimation. The nature of accident for estimating purposes is evaluated by vocational or rehabilitation experts, while the judgment date is suggested by the attorney requesting work.

Projection of Future Earnings

The projection of the plaintiff's future earnings requires determination of the plaintiff's worklife expectancy. **Worklife expectancy** is the number of years a person at a given age is expected to work or remain active in the labor force. The most popular source for the worklife expectancy is the *Worklife Estimates: Effects of Race and Education*, published by the U.S. Department of Labor, Bureau of Labor Statistics. In the publication, Life and Worklife Expectancies for Men by Race is used for male, while Life and Worklife Expectancies for Women by Race is used for female. When other tables are used, it usually means that the economist is attempting a slight gain in estimates by using a table that applies to a broader class of male or female.

Future earnings that the plaintiff would have earned without the accident are projected on the basis of the plaintiff's gross income records. Methods of projecting future earnings depend on how much earnings data the economist has and on the laws of the jurisdiction. Usually, the economist assumes either that the plaintiff's earnings growth during the past several years will continue, or that the plaintiff's earnings will increase in direct proportion to the growth rate of earnings of the entire economy or the particular industry in which the plaintiff worked.

The projection of future earnings is made exclusive of inflation. When dollar values are net of inflation, they are called real values. Dollar values unadjusted for inflation are called nominal or money values. It makes sense to use real income data rather than nominal income data, since inflation affects both sides of the equation. On the one hand, future income streams are higher because of inflation. On the other hand, future income streams should be discounted to the present value by a discount rate that is also higher because of inflation. Since inflation affects both sides equally, a simpler step would be to project future earnings net of inflation and use a discount rate net of inflation. One advantage of this approach is that there is no need for forecasting the rate of inflation. Discount rate adjusted for, or unaffected by, inflation is called the real discount rate or, in the legal circle, the **below-market discount rate**.

Discounting

Even in a world of no inflation, today's dollar is worth more than tomorrow's dollar because human beings value today's dollar more than tomorrow's dollar. Suppose that the plaintiff is judged to receive one dollar this year and another dollar one year from now. Suppose also that both dollars are paid to the plaintiff as a lump sum on the judgment day. Because of the smaller value of the next year's dollar, the plaintiff should not receive two dollars. Instead, the lump sum payment should be something less than two dollars. How much less depends on the discount rate.

If future values are discounted by a higher discount rate, their present values are smaller. If future values are discounted by a lower discount rate, their present values are larger although they are still smaller than future values. Attorneys working for the plaintiff prefer economists who use lower discount rates, while attorneys working for the defendant prefer economists who use higher discount rates. Although many economists believe that the real rate of interest is close to 2 or 3 percent, it is not uncommon that economists select time periods arbitrarily in such a way to benefit the particular client.

One interesting approach to the determination of a discount rate is the **total offset approach**, also known as the *Beaulieu* approach, in which the rate of increase of real wages is assumed to equal the real discount rate.[6] The total offset approach rests on the idea that the market rate of interest earned on the investment of a damage award will be adequately offset by price inflation and real wage increases. In the total offset approach, the base year earnings are multiplied by the plaintiff's worklife to obtain the damage award.

Adjustments

The present value of future earnings is obtained by summing the future earnings discounted to their present values. Before the damage estimate becomes final, several adjustments are made.

First, the value of fringe benefits is added to the present value before it becomes the damage estimate. **Fringe benefits** refer to payments beyond the basic salary that the defendant would have made to the injured without the accident. Fringe benefits include insurance coverage, pension and retirement plans, profit-sharing, and even in-kind services. A usual process of estimating fringe benefits is to treat them as a fixed percentage of base earnings. Second, income taxes are subtracted since the plaintiff would not have received these taxes even if there were no accident.

Third, unlike personal injury, personal death ends the life of the person represented by the plaintiff. Personal death causes the deceased person to no longer consume goods and services. A given jurisdiction, therefore, may allow the deceased person's expenditure to be deducted from the damage award.

Hedonic Damages

In recent years, some economists suggested that awards in wrongful death (and possibly injury) cases include compensation to the loss of the pleasure or enjoyment of life, known as **hedonic damages**. The real problem of whether or not awards should be made to compensate for the loss of the pleasure of life lies in developing a conceptual basis for the award that many can agree on. This development requires answers to numerous questions including: Why should the estate receive the award when the deceased cannot benefit? Do hedonic damage awards have anything to do with deterrence value? How are hedonic damage awards different from gratuitous home care services and the value of a housewife's domestic work? How are hedonic damages different from punitive damages? Although these questions are beyond the scope of this article,[7] a recent Supreme Court ruling allowed hedonic awards separately from punitive damages.[8]

According to Section 2674 of the Federal Tort Claims Act (FTCA), the United States is not liable for punitive damages. When the petitioner seeked under FTCA damage awards for the loss of enjoyment of life of her late husband, the government made a strict dichotomy between compensatory and punitive damages by claiming that damages that are not strictly compensatory are necessarily punitive damages barred by Section 2674. In reversing the District Court ruling that supported the government position, Justice Clarence Thomas states that "punitive damages" embodies an element of the defendant's conduct that must be proved before such damages are awarded. The common law recognizes that damages intended to compensate the plaintiff are different in kind from punitive damages. According to Justice Thomas, "Section 2674 prohibits awards of 'punitive damages,' not damage awards that may have a punitive effect."[9] Although the Supreme Court permitted damage awards for the loss of enjoyment of life under FTCA, the actual recovery is still subject to the laws of the jurisdiction.

Summary

The process of evaluating a profitability of major investment projects is known as capital budgeting. In the net present value approach, the present value of the cash flows from a projected investment obtained and the initial capital outlay is subtracted from the present value. The NPV method requires an estimation of future cash flows and the selection of a required rate of return for discounting of future cash flows. The internal rate of return is a discount rate that equates the present value of future cash flows to the initial cash outlay.

In capital budgeting, business managers either undertake feasibility studies or carry out the projects. The feasibility of a highway project is usually stated as a benefit cost ratio. Economic benefits have two components; transportation benefits and economic development benefits. Transportation benefits include the dollar value of savings in travel time for passenger vehicles as well as trucks, savings in operation and maintenance costs of vehicles, the dollar value of reduced fatality, and the dollar value of reduced non-fatal accidents. Development benefits include short-term benefits from expenditures of construction dollars and long-term economic development benefits. Economic costs of building the highway are the sum of labor and material costs of constructing the highway, right-of-way costs, periodic resurfacing costs, and reduced property tax revenue from right-of-way acquisitions.

Short-term economic development benefits are usually not counted as benefits, because construction dollars are opportunity costs that can easily be spent elsewhere generating comparable expenditure benefits. Long-term economic development benefits may or may not be included in estimation of benefits. At least, the portion of long-term benefits that exceed the average long-term development benefits when the same dollars are spent on all public sector projects should be included.

The benefit-cost ratio varies with the discount rate. The long-term real discount rate in the economy averages two to three percent. The suggestion made by OMB Circular A-94 to use a seven percent real discount rate in evaluating highway projects may cause the value of a highway to be underestimated, since highway projects tend to generate positive externalities that are seldom matched by other projects. Expenditures on public sector projects generate secondary expenditures impact, known as the multiplier effect. The multiplier effect is usually not included in estimating benefits of a new highway.

The most difficult part of a subdivision feasibility study is to estimate the market potential, or the absorption rate. It can be estimated by using data on population changes, percent of owner-occupied housing units, number of new homes built, and the relation between demand for lots and demand for new homes. Finally, a brief introduction of forensic economics is made in the last section in which the method of estimating the present value of future lost earnings is described. The method is employed extensively in personal injury and wrongful death cases.

Endnotes

1. Lawrence D. Schall, Gary L. Sundem, and William R. Geijsbeek, Jr., "Survey and Analysis of Capital Budgeting Methods," *Journal of Finance*, 33 (March 1978), 281-287.
2   Multicriteria evaluation covers a wide range of approaches. It may be a dynamic programming, which extends the least cost approach with a single objective to one with multi-objectives, or it may be an indexing and ranking approach. For details, see J. L. Cohen, and D. H. Marks, "Multiobjective screen models and water resource investment," *Water Resource Research*, 9 (August 1973), 826-836; and Jaimu Won, "Multicriteria Evaluation Approaches to Urban Transportation Projects," *Urban Studies*, 27 (February 1990), 119-138.
3. These studies include: Ronald Briggs, "Interstate Highway System and Development in Nonmetropolitan Areas," *Transportation Research Record 812*, 1981, pp. 9-12; Craig R. Humphrey, Craig R., and Ralph R. Sell, "The Impact of Controlled Access Highways on Population Growth in Pennsylvania Nonmetropolitan Communities, 1940-1970," *Rural Sociology*, 40 (Fall 1975), 332-343; John F. Kain, "Computer Simulation Models of Urban Location," in Edwin S. Mills, ed., *Handbook of Regional and Urban Economics*, Vol. 2 Urban Economics, Amsterdam: North-Holland, 1986, pp. 847-875; Kuehn, John A., and Jerry G. West, "Highways and Regional Development," *Growth and Change*, 2 (July 1991), 23-28; Putman, Stephen H., *Integrated Policy Analysis of Metropolitan Transportation and Location*, Washington, D.C.: U.S. Department of Transportation, Report DOT-P-30-80-32, August

1980; and Roehl, Wesley S., Julie Fesenmaier, and Daniel R. Fesenmaier, "Highway Accessibility and Regional Tourist Expenditures," *Journal of Travel Research*, 31 (Winter 1993), 58-63.

4. *Jones v. Laughlin*, 462 U.S. 523.
5. For details, see Semoon Chang, "Forensic Economics at Trial: Estimating Future Lost Earnings," *TRIAL*, 29 (April 1993), 63-66.
6. See for example 5(b) of the Longshoremen's and Harbor Workers' Compensation Act (33 USCS 905(b)). The seminal case of the total offset approach, however, is *Beaulieu v Elliott*, 434 P2d 665 (Alaska 1967).
7. Interested readers are suggested to read the Fall 1990 issue of the *Journal of Forensic Economics*, dedicated to hedonic damages and the value of life.
8. *Molzof v. U.S.*, 60 U.S.L.W. 4081 (1992 W: 2900 (U.S.)) decided January 14, 1992.
9. *Molzof v. U.S.*, 60 U.S.L.W. 4082.

Table 1. Student's t Distribution

Degrees of Freedom	Probability of a Value Greater in Absolute Value than the Table Entry					
	0.01	0.02	0.05	0.1	0.2	0.3
1	63.657	31.821	12.706	6.314	3.078	1.963
2	9.925	6.965	4.303	2.920	1.886	1.386
3	5.841	4.541	3.182	2.353	1.638	1.250
4	4.604	3.747	2.776	2.132	1.533	1.190
5	4.032	3.365	2.571	2.015	1.476	1.156
6	3.707	3.143	2.447	1.943	1.440	1.134
7	3.499	2.998	2.365	1.895	1.415	1.119
8	3.355	2.896	2.306	1.860	1.397	1.108
9	3.250	2.821	2.262	1.833	1.383	1.100
10	3.169	2.764	2.228	1.812	1.372	1.093
11	3.106	2.718	2.201	1.796	1.363	1.088
12	3.055	2.681	2.179	1.782	1.356	1.083
13	3.012	2.650	2.160	1.771	1.350	1.079
14	2.977	2.624	2.145	1.761	1.345	1.076
15	2.947	2.602	2.131	1.753	1.341	1.074
16	2.921	2.583	2.120	1.746	1.337	1.071
17	2.898	2.567	2.110	1.740	1.333	1.069
18	2.878	2.552	2.101	1.734	1.330	1.067
19	2.861	2.539	2.093	1.729	1.328	1.066
20	2.845	2.528	2.086	1.725	1.325	1.064
21	2.831	2.518	2.080	1.721	1.323	1.063
22	2.819	2.508	2.074	1.717	1.321	1.061
23	2.807	2.500	2.069	1.714	1.319	1.060
24	2.797	2.492	2.064	1.711	1.318	1.059
25	2.787	2.485	2.060	1.708	1.316	1.058
26	2.779	2.479	2.056	1.706	1.315	1.058
27	2.771	2.473	2.052	1.703	1.314	1.057
28	2.763	2.467	2.048	1.701	1.313	1.056
29	2.756	2.462	2.045	1.699	1.311	1.055
30	2.750	2.457	2.042	1.697	1.310	1.055
x	2.576	2.326	1.960	1.645	1.282	1.036

Source: Reprinted from Table IV in Sir Ronald A. Fisher, *Statistical Methods for Research Workers*, 13th edition, Oliver & Boyd Ltd., Edinburgh, 1963.

Table 2. Five Percent Significance Points of d_L and d_U in Two-Tailed Tests

n	k'=1		k'=2		k'=3		k'=4		k'=5	
	d_L	d_U	d_L	d_U	d_L	d_U	d_L	d_U	d_L	d_U
15	0.95	1.23	0.83	1.40	0.71	1.61	0.59	1.84	0.48	2.09
16	0.98	1.24	0.86	1.40	0.75	1.59	0.64	1.80	0.53	2.03
17	1.01	1.25	0.90	1.40	0.79	1.58	0.68	1.77	0.57	1.98
18	1.03	1.26	0.93	1.40	0.82	1.56	0.72	1.74	0.62	1.93
19	1.06	1.28	0.96	1.41	0.86	1.55	0.76	1.72	0.66	1.90
20	1.08	1.28	0.99	1.41	0.89	1.55	0.79	1.70	0.70	1.87
21	1.10	1.30	1.01	1.41	0.92	1.54	0.83	1.69	0.73	1.84
22	1.12	1.31	1.04	1.42	0.95	1.54	0.86	1.68	0.77	1.82
23	1.14	1.32	1.06	1.42	0.97	1.54	0.89	1.67	0.80	1.80
24	1.16	1.33	1.08	1.43	1.00	1.54	0.91	1.66	0.83	1.79
25	1.18	1.34	1.10	1.43	1.02	1.54	0.94	1.65	0.86	1.77
26	1.19	1.35	1.12	1.44	1.04	1.54	0.96	1.65	0.88	1.76
27	1.21	1.36	1.13	1.44	1.06	1.54	0.99	1.64	0.91	1.75
28	1.22	1.37	1.15	1.45	1.08	1.54	1.01	1.64	0.93	1.74
29	1.24	1.38	1.17	1.45	1.10	1.54	1.03	1.63	0.96	1.73
30	1.25	1.38	1.18	1.46	1.12	1.54	1.05	1.63	0.98	1.73
31	1.26	1.39	1.20	1.47	1.13	1.55	1.07	1.63	1.00	1.72
32	1.27	1.40	1.21	1.47	1.15	1.55	1.08	1.63	1.02	1.71
33	1.28	1.41	1.22	1.48	1.16	1.55	1.10	1.63	1.04	1.71
34	1.29	1.41	1.24	1.48	1.17	1.55	1.12	1.63	1.06	1.70
35	1.30	1.42	1.25	1.48	1.19	1.55	1.13	1.63	1.07	1.70
36	1.31	1.43	1.26	1.49	1.20	1.56	1.15	1.63	1.09	1.70
37	1.32	1.43	1.27	1.49	1.21	1.56	1.16	1.62	1.10	1.70
38	1.33	1.44	1.28	1.50	1.23	1.56	1.17	1.62	1.12	1.70
39	1.34	1.44	1.29	1.50	1.24	1.56	1.19	1.63	1.13	1.69
40	1.35	1.45	1.30	1.51	1.25	1.57	1.20	1.63	1.15	1.69
45	1.39	1.48	1.34	1.53	1.30	1.58	1.25	1.63	1.21	1.69
50	1.42	1.50	1.38	1.54	1.34	1.59	1.30	1.64	1.26	1.69
55	1.45	1.52	1.41	1.56	1.37	1.60	1.33	1.64	1.30	1.69
60	1.47	1.54	1.44	1.57	1.40	1.61	1.37	1.65	1.33	1.69
65	1.49	1.55	1.46	1.59	1.43	1.62	1.40	1.66	1.36	1.69
70	1.51	1.57	1.48	1.60	1.45	1.63	1.42	1.66	1.39	1.70
75	1.53	1.58	1.50	1.61	1.47	1.64	1.45	1.67	1.42	1.70
80	1.54	1.59	1.52	1.62	1.49	1.65	1.47	1.67	1.44	1.70
85	1.56	1.60	1.53	1.63	1.51	1.65	1.49	1.68	1.46	1.71
90	1.57	1.61	1.55	1.64	1.53	1.66	1.50	1.69	1.48	1.71
95	1.58	1.62	1.56	1.65	1.54	1.67	1.52	1.69	1.50	1.71
100	1.59	1.63	1.57	1.65	1.55	1.67	1.53	1.70	1.51	1.72

Source: J. Durbin and G.S. Watson, "Testing for Serial Correlation in Least Squares Regression," *Biometrika*, 38 (1951), pp. 159-177.

INDEX

Author's Bio-sketch

Semoon Chang has received his batchelor's degree from Seoul National University, master's degree from Southern Illinois University, and Ph. D. degree in economics from Florida State University. He is currently professor of economics as well as director of the Center for Business and Economic Research at the University of South Alabama.

Dr. Chang has provided numerous consulting services to both public agencies and private businesses, which include local governments, engineering firms, land developers, utility companies, tourism agencies, and attorneys. His articles, notes, and letters of correspondence have been published in such journals as *Growth and Change, Governmental Finance, Journal of Business Strategies, Journal of Economic Perspectives, Journal of Travel Research, Labor Law Review, Oil & Gas Tax Quarterly, Real Estate Law Journal, Southern Economic Journal, Transportation Journal, Trial, University of West Los Angeles Law Review, Urban Affairs Quarterly,* and others. His previous books have been published by Allyn & Bacon, Prentice-Hall, and University Press of America.